THE
ALGARVE
—in your pocket—

MICHELIN®

MAIN CONTRIBUTOR: Paul Murphy

PHOTOGRAPH CREDITS
Photos supplied by The Travel Library: A Amsel
title page, 77, 90; Stuart Black front cover, back cover,
7, 8, 11, 12, 16, 17, 19, 21, 23, 24, 25 (t, b), 26, 27, 28,
29, 31, 32, 33, 34, 36, 38, 40, 41, 42, 44, 45, 47, 48, 49,
50, 51, 52, 53, 54, 56, 58, 59, 60, 61, 62, 63, 64, 65, 67,
68, 70, 71, 73, 74, 75, 78, 79, 81, 83, 84, 87, 88, 93, 96,
98, 100, 102, 104, 105, 109, 111, 117, 118, 121, 123, 124,
126; Roger Howard 5, 55, 86, 107; Gordon Lethbridge
114.
Other photos: Nature Photographers/Andrew Cleave
30.

*Front cover: Praia do Camilo, near Lagos; back cover: fishing
boats, Carvoeiro; title page: girl in traditional costume*

MANUFACTURE FRANÇAISE DES PNEUMATIQUES MICHELIN

Société en commandite par actions au capital de 2 000 000 000 de francs

Place des Carmes-Déchaux – 63 Clermont-Ferrand (France)

R.C.S. Clermont-Fd 855 200 507

© Michelin et Cie. Propriétaires-Éditeurs 1997

Dépôt légal Mai 97 – ISBN 2-06-651701-1 – ISSN en cours

Printed in Spain 4-97

CONTENTS

INTRODUCTION

The Algarve is unquestionably one of the great late-20C European playgrounds. First and foremost is its 150km (90 mile) Atlantic coastline of golden beaches, with its western section backed by magnificent cliff scenery. Its climate offers comfortably hot summers and balmy winters, and first-class sports facilities flourish. A high standard of accommodation is still found at reasonable prices, and the Portuguese people are reserved but friendly and charming hosts.

But is there really any more to the Algarve than lying on a picturesque beach or swinging a golf club? Although major historical sights are few and far between, the splendid castle of Silves and the old parts of Faro, Tavira and Lagos are testament to a nation which during the 16C led the world in exploration and trade. Since those heady days, however, their forebears have suffered many vicissitudes and, away from the resorts, the Algarve remains very rural. Here, little has changed in decades. Agriculture still dominates the economy, and the pace of life is slow. You will still see old ladies wearing traditional black bonnets, old men in tall black felt hats, and donkeys and carts trundling along back roads. And even on the coast, right next to the bronzing bodies, brightly painted fishing boats still haul up and disgorge their catch, oblivious to camera-toting tourists. It is these vignettes of a slowly disappearing lifestyle that give the Algarve its identity and character.

So make the most of your stay in Portugal's deep south; enjoy the beach, the weather and the sport, but also take a step back – get off the beaten track, and experience the traditional Algarve.

Striking coastal scenery and wide sandy beaches have made the Algarve one of the most popular regions in Europe.

BACKGROUND

GEOGRAPHY

The Algarve, Europe's south-western extremity, is roughly rectangular in shape, 150km (90 miles) east to west, and approximately 30-40km (18-24 miles) north to south. It is bounded by the Atlantic to the south and west, by the River Guadiana (marking the Spanish border) to the east, and by the province of Alentejo to the north.

The coastal strip divides neatly into two: the Barlavento (windward) coast, just west of Faro, and the Sotavento (leeward) coast, east of Faro. The former offers the classic Algarve scenery of picture-postcard beaches and red-ochre sandstone cliffs, weathered by wind and wave into fantastically shaped stacks and grottoes. To the east there are no cliffs, but the sand is just as good.

Behind the resorts is a series of ranges, which reach a peak of 902m (2 959ft) at Fóia. These are dotted with forests of oak, chestnut, beech, cork and eucalyptus. The latter has been introduced in recent years to provide pulp for the paper industry, but the presence of this thirsty evergreen has exacerbated the region's water shortage problems. Hotels and golf courses which have sunk deep wells for fresh water are other culprits, and there are real fears that the long-term effects will be detrimental to the Algarve's verdant landscape.

The region also has two important wetland areas: the Ria Formosa lagoon system, which includes a number of inhabited barrier islands; and the Reserva do Sapal at Castro Marim. The Algarve's two major rivers are the Arade, which meets the sea at Portimão, and the Rio Guadiana. There is also a number of large semi-natural reservoirs (*barragens*).

HISTORY

Early Origins

The first permanent inhabitants of the Algarve were the **Cyretes**, who occupied the land after the **Phoenicians** and the **Carthaginians** had established trading posts here. There is evidence of **Greek** occupation too, but the first invaders to leave any lasting mark were the **Romans**, who named the province (comprising most of present-day Portugal) Lusitania. In the 3C they brought

Beyond the beach resorts of the Algarve is a delightful rural hinterland.

7

This fish mosaic from the baths at the Roman ruins at Milreu illustrates Portugal's age-old link to the sea.

Christianity to Lusitania, and the region's first bishop had his seat at Faro. Mosaics in Faro and remains nearby at Milreu attest to a high standard of living, while the bridge at Tavira is a legacy of the Romans' famous civil engineering skills.

The Moors

Following the decline of the Roman Empire, the Algarve fell to the **Visigoths** of northern Europe in the 5C. Later, in AD 711, the Iberian peninsula was overrun by the **Moorish armies** of North Africa, during which time the Algarve received its name, deriving from the Arabic *El-Gharb*, meaning 'The Land to the West'.

The capital of the Algarve was Chelb (or Xelb), today known as Silves, but the province was ruled from Seville. Southern Portuguese society was as enlightened, tolerant and cultured as that of southern Spain, and for nearly 500 years the region was prosperous and largely peaceful. During this same period, however, the **Christian forces** in the north were planning the **Reconquista** (Reconquest), and slowly fought their way south, chipping away at the Moorish empire. Silves was sacked in 1189, and although it was briefly retaken by the Moors soon afterwards, Moorish domination came to an end in 1249 with the final Reconquest of the Algarve in Faro.

Today, the magnificent red sandstone castle of Silves is the most tangible reminder of the Moors, though their legacy pervades modern society in many ways: citrus crops, almonds, the small white cube-like houses, filigree chimney stacks, many arts and crafts (including *azulejos, see* p.18), and the Algarve sweet tooth are all inherited from the Moors.

The following century witnessed the stabilisation and strengthening of the country, thanks in large part to the leadership of its king, Dom Dinis (1279-1325). The spectre of Castilian domination overshadowed Portugal, however, and after many years of political intrigue, a two-year war was fought. The **Battle of Aljubarrota** (*see* photo p.52) in 1385 saw the Portuguese victorious and peace was finally agreed in 1411, leaving Portugal free to consider its own plans for expanding her empire and entering a Golden Age.

Henry the Navigator and the Age of Exploration

The architect of Portugal's Golden Age was Prince Henry 'the Navigator' (1394-1460), son of King João I and his English wife, Philippa of Lancaster. Henry was no soldier, nor even a sailor, but he was a superb organiser and an inspirational leader. In 1415 his first military action, the capture of Ceuta, in Morocco, was a spectacular success.

Driven by a thirst for knowledge and a zealot's mission to roll back the frontiers of Christianity, Henry devoted himself to exploration. A prince, and also Grand Master of the Order of Christ (the successors to the Knights Templar), he used his considerable wealth and influence to assemble the greatest nautical minds of the day. Cartographers, navigators and shipbuilders were summoned to Sagres, then known as Vila do Infante (the Prince's Town), to chart new routes, to build new ships, and to explore uncharted waters. They succeeded in redesigning the caravel into the most effective sailing ship of its day and in 1419, with the help of new navigational methods, they discovered Madeira. In 1427 the Azores were sighted, later the Cape Verde islands, and before long large parts of the west coast of Africa were colonised.

Despite his successes, Henry seems to have had few pleasures, leading a life of abstinence and piety. Nevertheless, it seems he remained oblivious, in typical medieval style, to the terrible suffering his slavery-funded voyages were causing. Henry died in 1460, in massive debt from the cost of his ventures, but his torch was carried by two more great Portuguese explorers.

In 1487, Bartolomeu Dias became the first European to round the tip of Africa, naming it Cabo da Boa Esperança (Cape of Good Hope) and, before the century was out, Vasco da Gama had found Henry's Holy Grail – the trade route to the Indies. Riches from

African gold and slaves, and spices and treasures from the Indies propelled Portugal to superpower status. In 1500 Brazil was discovered, and by the mid-16C Portugal dominated world trade, with empire staging posts as far apart as Goa, Malacca, Hormuz and Macau.

A statue of Henry the Navigator in Lagos.

The End of the Golden Age

The fabulous riches which poured into the Portuguese coffers during the late 15C and early 16C were squandered by an extravagant royalty, who not only neglected the country's infrastructure but deprived it of its finest commercial talents when they expelled the Jews in 1496. Domestic productivity fell and so, unfortunately, did international spice prices, yet the costs of maintaining the empire continued to spiral. In 1578, Portugal launched her last and most disastrous venture abroad. **Dom Sebastião,** a charismatic boy-king, filled with a pathological hatred of the Moors, set sail from Lagos at the head of a 15 000-strong army to conquer Morocco. Ill-equipped and badly led, the Portuguese were

This azulejos bench in Olhão shows the discovery of Rio de Janiero, at the beginning of the 16C.

overwhelmed on the sands of **El-Ksar El-Kebir**. It is estimated that the Portuguese body count was some 8 000 men, and fewer than 100 escaped capture. The ransom demanded for the survivors almost bankrupted the country, and the death of the boy-king on the battlefield left Portugal with no legitimate heir.

Spain watched the worsening situation with glee, and in 1581 **King Philip II of Spain** (Dom Sebastião's uncle) sealed his claim to the Portuguese throne at the **Battle of Alcântara**. This new forced alliance with Spain brought several much needed economic benefits. However, it also meant enmity with the English and the Dutch, Spain's rivals for world supremacy, and for this the Algarve suffered.

In 1587 **Sir Francis Drake** sacked Sagres, and in 1596 English ships destroyed Faro. Abroad, Portugal's empire was being eroded by its new enemies, while at home conditions under its overlord worsened. Meanwhile, Spain was facing troubles of its own, with domestic strife and a war with France. In 1640, the Portuguese staged a palace coup and installed the **Bragança** dynasty.

Diamonds and Disaster

With Spain diverted, Portugal began to rebuild its economy, reforging its old British alliance with the marriage of **Catarina de Bragança** to **Charles II**. The country's coffers received a great boost during the late 17C, when gold and diamonds were discovered in Brazil, but once again its rulers wasted enormous sums.

On All Saints' Day, 1 November 1755, tragedy struck Portugal and, above all, the

Algarve. **The Great Earthquake**, as it came to
be known, is thought to have had its
epicentre just off the Atlantic coast, between
Faro and Tavira. A massive tidal wave surged
over the province, killing some 5 000
people, many of them in church. Fires raged
uncontrollably, and hardly a building of
significance survived. Over the following
years, it is thought that some 50 000 people
from the Algarve, the Alentejo, and even as
far as Lisbon may have died from secondary
injuries and from the effects of famine and
disease wrought by the disaster.

Wars and Republicanism
The 19C once again saw the country
enmeshed in Europe's power struggles. The
Spanish invaded in 1801, marking the
beginning of the **War of the Oranges**, and
then the French demanded support from
the Portuguese in their blockade of the
British. The Portuguese refused to help
France, so in 1807 **Napoleon** invaded and
stayed for four years. In 1811 a coalition of
forces from Britain, Portugal and Spain (the
latter also being under the Napoleonic
yoke), led by the Duke of Wellington, finally
succeeded in expelling the French. Britain's
reward for its help was to be allowed to trade
direct with Brazil, putting an end to
Portugal's lucrative role as intermediary.

The Portuguese monarchy was by now in
dire straits. During the War of the Oranges,
the family had fled to Brazil. When, in 1822,
Brazil declared independence, **Pedro IV**,
king of Portugal, decided to stay on as
Emperor of Brazil, and to transfer
responsibility for the homeland to his
brother, **Miguel**. He arranged for Miguel to
become the king of Portugal on condition

that he should accept a constitutional charter of liberal reforms. However, once empowered, Miguel reneged on the charter and provoked the **War of the Two Brothers**. With the aid of the British, Pedro defeated Miguel in 1833. This was far from the end of the problem, however, and the rest of the century witnessed growing dissatisfaction with the monarchy and the resulting rise of **Republicanism**.

The first coup in 1908 failed, despite the assassination of King Dom Carlos and his son. However, in 1910 King Dom Manuel was finally ousted and exiled to England, and Portugal was declared a republic.

The Republic

Between 1910 and 1926 the new state was in chaos, changing government an astonishing 45 times. **General Carmona** was appointed president when one of many military interventions finally caused the republican constitution to be suspended. In 1932 **António de Oliveira Salazar** became Prime Minister, and instituted a virtual dictatorship which was to last until 1968. During the latter part of this period, Portugal suffered the cost of colonial wars and international disapproval, while yearning for liberalist policies. Finally, in 1974, Salazar's successor, **Marcelo Caetano**, was removed in a bloodless army coup.

The following period saw the loss of the remaining colonies, at a terrible cost in terms of refugees, but also a general stabilisation of political and economic affairs. **Mário Soares** was appointed in 1986 as Portugal's first civilian president for 60 years, and in the same year the country entered into the European Union.

The Algarve, which has been successfully attracting mass tourism since the 1970s, has also benefited enormously from injections of EU cash, and will probably continue to do so into the 21C. Meanwhile, although Portugal is still one of Europe's poorest countries, its immediate future is looking bright.

THE PEOPLE AND CULTURE

The people of the Algarve have a slow, gentle charm, which will come as a pleasant surprise to visitors more used to the fiery panache and bravado which is often displayed by their Iberian neighbours across the Rio Guadiana.

First, though, you will have to meet the locals. The waiters in tourist hotels and restaurants may well be from Lisbon or elsewhere, and there is hardly a local to be

Locals in Salir passing the time of day.

A fishing boat chugs home past a sail-boat after a hard day's work. Fishing and tourism are the mainstays of the Algarve's economy.

found in the expensive 'Sportugal' resorts which lie between Faro and Albufeira. So, where to go? Try the tourist-free nightlife scene in Faro, the ebullient fish market in Olhão, or a busy local café anywhere off the tourist track.

It is said that one of the national characteristics is *saudade*, a melancholic nostalgia, best expressed in *fado* singing (*see* p.104). Given the country's turbulent recent history, this is perhaps an understandable emotion in the older generations.

Do not be misled, however, into stereotyping all Portuguese as sad-eyed dreamers – the new generation of Portuguese youth have rediscovered something of the adventurous spirit of their forebears.

The Decorative Arts

Azulejos

Portugal's most famous example of decorative art is the use of *azulejos*, which may be seen all over the Algarve. The pronunciation is (roughly) ah-zoo-lay'-joosh (with a soft *j* in the final syllable). The derivation of the word is either from the Arabic *azraq* (blue), the Portuguese *azul* (blue), and/or the Arabic *az-zulay/al-zuleich*, meaning small polished stone.

The term *azulejo* may refer to a single painted glazed tile, or to a whole wall or series of pictorial or patterned glazed tiles. They are common in nearly every public place (street signs, benches, churches) and are also used as marks of prestige (e.g., at Estói Palace). The Moors originated the art, although it was not until the 15C that *azulejos* were introduced to Portugal from Seville by Moorish craftsmen. Many historic tiles in the Algarve date from between the late 17C and early 18C, when the fashion was for exclusively blue-and-white tiles. The most striking examples of this kind are at the Igreja de São Lourenço near Almansil, the cathedral at Faro and the parish church at Alte. The *azulejo*-decorated benches at Largo 1° de Dezembro, Portimão, are possibly the most enjoyable and informative of all, reducing Portuguese history to ten easy pieces. For polychromatic patterns, see the beautiful examples at Estói, or, on a much less grand scale, the *trompe l'oeil* picture tiles in the parish church of Alvor. If you want to take some *azulejos* home with you, visit Porches.

The Manueline Style

Manueline architecture is uniquely Portuguese. It is named after King Manuel I, during whose reign (1495-1521) the style was developed, and it celebrates the age of maritime discoveries. Thus motifs of anchors, knotted ropes, sails, marine plants and creatures were used by stonemasons and architects during this period. The best examples of the Manueline style in the Algarve are the church portals at Silves, Monchique, São Bartolomeu de Messines and Alvor.

Azulejos tiles in the Church of St Anthony, Lagos (see p.59).

TS

SEE

ve is a small region, so you should be able to explore the following places comfortably during a two-week holiday, and still have plenty of time just to laze in the sun on one of the Algarve's famous beaches – the primary attraction for most tourists.

Albufeira
Brash, commercialised and crowded it may be, but it also boasts some of the best beaches on the coast (particularly those just to the west) and, for the 18–30-something crowd, the best nightlife too.

Alte
The Algarve's prettiest village is popular with locals as well as tourists. Enjoy a Sunday barbecue or picnic by the springs, and do not miss the young folk dancers in the evening at the Fonte Pequena.

Around Carvoeiro
Head east of Carvoeiro to find some of the area's most perfect coves before the developers get there.

Faro
Take a stroll in the cobbled Old Town, and stop for refreshments in the Café Aliança (a favourite with the locals), or enjoy a night out in Faro's restaurants and bars, and you will discover that this, the regional capital, is one of the Algarve's best-kept secrets.

Lagos
Fabulous beaches and coves, an historic town, and an exuberant (though not overly intrusive) nightlife, combine to make Lagos one of the best destinations on the coast.

The attractive harbour of Faro is built at the edge of a wide lagoon.

Ponta de Sagres and Cabo de São Vicente

Henry the Navigator planned his historic voyages at Ponta de Sagres, and until his daring team set forth, this forlorn spot was considered to be Land's End. Visit in the evening to experience the magical sunsets.

Portimão and Praia da Rocha

With its stunning beach, it is easy to see why Praia da Rocha is a popular resort. Sardines on the quay is an Algarve institution. They may actually *taste* as good elsewhere, but Portimão's dockside, with its hustle, bustle and raw energy, imparts a flavour all its own.

21

Serra de Monchique

The hills and scenery of Monchique provide a breath of fresh air after the languor of the coast. Do not miss the medicinal springs at Caldas de Monchique, or the views from the road to Aljezur.

Silves

The old Moorish capital dreams of the past. Its castle is the finest in the region.

Tavira

The architecture and town planning of Tavira provides a striking contrast to the 'costa resorts'. Spend a relaxed morning here, then take a boat to its sandbar beach, Ilha de Tavira.

FARO

Faro is the capital of the Algarve, and its airport provides the international gateway to the region. Most visitors simply pass the town by, preferring the pleasures of resort life. Those who choose to spend some time here find a typical Portuguese small town: busy and workaday, but very welcoming, with cafés set around small squares, a harbour, and enough historical interest for at least a full day. Independent travellers, staying a night or two, might like to take a small boat to one of its off-shore beaches, and later sample the lively local nightlife.

The Old Town

The historical heart of Faro is the Old Town, a charming peaceful cobbled quarter, entered by the **Arco da Vila**, a handsome 18C neoclassical arch, topped by a bell tower, complete with nesting storks. (Next to the Arco you will find the tourist office.)

Dominating the Old Town is the **Sé** (cathedral), a cavernous, mostly Gothic edifice with some outstanding *azulejos* (tiles). Its square, Largo da Sé, is a handsome sight, ringed with orange trees. Almost hidden behind the Sé lies the graceful **Convento de Nossa Senhora da Assunção** (Convent of Our Lady of the Ascension), with its beautiful cloister. It now houses the Museu Municipal (Municipal Museum), with a fine archaeological collection, including a large, well-preserved Roman mosaic and *azulejos*.

The **Galeria do Trem** is worth visiting for its exhibits of contemporary artists. Elsewhere is the occasional shop, restaurant and café, but the Old Town, with its charming cobbled backstreets, is a place for a quiet stroll among some fine architecture.

The simple interior of Faro's cathedral is cool and spacious.

23

The cloister of the former Convent of Our Lady of the Ascension. The convent now houses the Municipal Museum.

The 'New Town' and Faro Outskirts

Stop for a coffee in the pleasant **Jardim Manuel Bivar** (Manuel Bivar Gardens) next to the Arco da Vila, then follow Rua Francisco Gomes to the lively, pedestrianised Rua de Santo António. Much of the buzz and everyday activity of Faro is to be found along (and just off) this main shopping thoroughfare. Continue on to find the **Museu de Etnografia Regional** (Regional Ethnographic Museum), which provides a glimpse of the traditional Algarve way of life.

At the harbour is the **Museu Marítimo** (Maritime Museum), with a good collection of model ships illustrating Faro's fishing and naval history. It is only comparatively recently, with the silting of its harbour, that Faro ceased to be a port open to the Atlantic. In 1596, the English fleet was able to sail right up to the city walls, to pillage and torch the Spanish-ruled town.

Dotted around Faro are a number of handsome churches. Best of all is the Baroque **Igreja do Carmo** (Carmelite Church) notable for its rich interior, but much more famous for its curious and

The interesting exhibits at Faro's Maritime Museum have explanations in English.

This striking mosaic paving leads up to Faro's Carmelite Church, with its unusual Chapel of Bones.

macabre **Capela dos Ossos** (Chapel of Bones), constructed in the early 19C. Here, over 1 200 skulls and bones from monks and local parishioners have been used as building materials, in a grim memorial to Man's mortality.

Overlooking Faro, the church belfry known as **Miradouro de Santo António** (St Anthony's Lookout Point) offers a beautiful sweeping **panorama** across the bay. There is also a museum dedicated to St Anthony in the courtyard below.

One of the region's few stately homes to escape the devastation of 1755 (*see* p.13) is

The romantic gardens of the Palace of Estói are adorned with lovely decorative features, such as these azulejos staircases.

Very little remains of the temple of the I C AD Roman town of Ossonoba, at Milreu.

the **Palácio de Estói** (Palace of Estói), 9km (14.5 miles) north of Faro. Sadly, the Baroque interior is closed to the public. The formal gardens, although rather dilapidated, are adorned with bougainvillaea, balustraded terraces, marble busts and colourful *azulejos*, giving them a dreamy Alice-in-Wonderland atmosphere. At nearby **Milreu** are the knee-high ruins of a Roman patrician house, with a few floor mosaics, hinting at bygone splendour (*see* illustration p.8). The adjacent structure is the remains of a 4C Roman temple.

THE SOTAVENTO COAST

The Sotavento (leeward) coast is the lesser known, less spectacular eastern half of the Algarve. It may lack the scenic drama of the west coast, but it still offers plenty of interest, from salty Olhão to stately Tavira and the tranquillity of the beautiful Rio Guadiana.

Fishermen in Olhão mending their nets.

Olhão to Tavira

Olhão, 'the little white town of the Algarve', is famous for its cube-like fishermen's houses. On top of these houses are terraces with narrow outside staircases leading up and down, rather like one of M C Escher's famous mind-boggling drawings. Many have now gone, but look up and you can still find some, particularly in the side streets of the fishermen's quarter, just set back from the seafront. Here you will also find the busy, colourful **fishmarket**. Some of the fish are still landed here by small boats (though the main port lies just to the east), and *bacalhau* are pegged on lines to dry in the sun. Small boats carry visitors to and from the tiny barrier islands of **Armona** and **Culatra**, both of which offer beautiful sandy beaches.

The pedestrianised centre of Olhão is reminiscent of Faro, and at the imposing **Igreja Matriz** (parish church) you can climb the tower for bird's-eye **views**. Note the adjacent **Capela de Nossa Senhora dos Aflitos** (Chapel of Our Lady of the Suffering), where effigies of various parts of the human anatomy are placed as votive offerings, in the hope of relief or cure. Also in front of the church is the small **Museu de Olhão** ethnographic museum.

Offerings in the form of parts of the body are placed in the Chapel of Our Lady of the Suffering, in Olhão.

Just east of Olhão, look for the small sign to the interpretive centre of the **Parque Natural da Ria Formosa**. This important ecological site, which stretches from west of Quinta do Lago (*see* p.36) to Manta Rota (*see* p.32), is a permanently shifting lagoon system with barrier islands. At the interpretive centre you can peer into aquariums, take a self-guided walking tour round the salt pans, tidal mill and chameleon habitat, or enjoy some excellent birdwatching. The park is also home to the **Algarve waterdog** (*cão de água*), a rare and curious breed of poodle which has developed webbed feet to cope with the marshy terrain, and which once used to help the local fishermen with fetching and carrying tasks.

The Ria Formosa Natural Park contains important wildlife habitats, including extensive salt pans.

Tavira

Tavira is the Algarve's most elegant town. Dating mainly from the 18C, it has a plethora of fine mansions, elegant churches, abundant gardens and an almost total absence of modern developments. During the summer, classical music is piped into the river-front gardens and streets. Start your tour at the ruined **Castelo dos Mouros** (Moorish Castle), where only the 13C walls remain, enclosing beautiful gardens. The views from here, over a roofscape little changed in three or more centuries, are splendid. Adjacent is the **Igreja da Santa Maria do Castelo** (Church of St Mary of the Castle), the last resting place of the city's hero, Dom Paio Peres Correia, who retook the city from the Moors in 1242. There are many more fine churches around the town, but they are usually open during services only. The beautiful 16C **Igreja da Misericórdia**, just a few yards away, is well

The arched Roman bridge over the Rio Gilão links the two parts of the stately town of Tavira.

The Church of Misericórdia provides an atmospheric setting for the concerts which are often held here.

The Church of Misericórdia provides an atmospheric setting for the concerts which are often held here.

worth a visit (next door is the tourist office – ask here about church opening times).

The Rio Gilão divides the town, and is spanned by a seven-arched **bridge** which dates back to the Roman period. Come in the morning when a lively **market** lines the south bank. Do stroll across to the other side of the old bridge, if only to visit the garden square of **Praça Dr António Padinha**. Further along the river, boats depart to the barrier island of **Ilha de Tavira**, where there are good beaches.

Tavira to the Spanish Border

The coast east of Tavira has largely been colonised by the resorts of **Manta Rota** and **Monte Gordo**. The latter – small-scale, with a beach backed by dunes and pines – is by far preferable to the former. Aside from its long

Fishing boats in Monte Gordo.

lat beach, Monte Gordo's only claim to ame is its casino.

Vila Real de Santo António is the easternmost point of the Algarve, but its grandeur falls well short of the promise of its name. The only point of sightseeing interest is the **Praça do Marquês de Pombal**, a handsome square laid out in the 18C, distinguished by a black and white clock-shaped pattern which radiates out from a central obelisk. Pop into the small **Manuel Cabanas Museum** on the square to see a good collection of woodcuts.

A ferry makes the short journey to **Ayamonte**, on the Spanish side of the river, where the atmosphere is altogether more animated, and worth experiencing, particularly in the early evening. (You may be asked for your passport.)

Along the Border

The Rio Guadiana has formed a natural southern border between Portugal and southern Spain ever since the days when they were known by their old Roman names of Lusitania and Baetica. The two countries have always regarded each other with suspicion and sometimes hostility, so it is no wonder that there are castles overlooking the river.

The town of **Castro Marim**, just north of Vila Real, boasts two castles, though today little remains of either. The town's heyday came after the Reconquest when, according to the inscription on the entrance, Prince Henry the Navigator lived in the 13C **castle** high above the town. Today, it is given over to the altogether more peaceful pursuit of nature conservation, housing a small

The town of Castro Marim has a long history; the 13C castle can be seen in the background.

information office for the **Castro Marim Reserva do Sapal** (Marshland Reserve), which is rich in birdlife. There is also a small museum here. Below is the town's other fortification, the 17C **Fortaleza de São Sebastião** (St Sebastian's Fortress), of which only the walls survive.

As the Rio Guadiana winds its way north, it becomes more and more picturesque. You can take a river cruise from Vila Real, but a new road has been built so motorists can also appreciate its beauty. After a few kilometres of hilly, winding, narrow roads, the river beckons at the hamlet of **Foz de Odeleite**. It's a gorgeous pastoral scene of green groves, yellow fields and red earth descending to a broad bright blue ribbon. Sailing boats and the occassional *finca* (farmstead) on the Spanish side complete the picture. It is hard to believe that just a few kilometres to the south are crowded beaches.

FARO TO CARVOEIRO

The region immediately west of Faro has been dubbed 'Sportugal', and is chiefly famous for its exclusive sporting facilities. The high-density resort and sprawling satellites of Albufeira dominate the central part of the coast, and nowhere along this stretch escapes the tourist influence. West of Falésia begins the stunning coastline for which the Algarve is renowned.

Faro to Quarteira

The first point of interest west of Faro (16km/10 miles) is the **Igreja de São Lourenço** (Church of St Lawrence), stranded on a hill between the busy N 125 and the nearby village of Almansil. Its interior is decorated with some of the finest examples of *azulejos* (*see* p.18) in the Algarve most of which date from around 1730.

From dusty Almansil, side roads descend to the sea and fork left and right respectively to two of the Algarve's most prestigious holiday developments, **Quinta do Lago** and **Vale do Lobo**. The former is the most exclusive and more attractive, planned on an expansive scale to give its guests maximum space and privacy. The comprehensive sports facilities and luxurious restaurants of both complexes are open to monied day visitors, and the lovely

beach of Praia do Ancão and the Ria Formosa Natural Park at Quinta do Lago (*see* p.30) provide excellent free recreation.

A short way along the coast, **Quarteira** is a cheap and cheerful contrast to affluent Quinta do Lago. For a long time, the town's half-finished concrete canyons were the perfect example of the hotch-potch style of boomtown Algarvian resort planning (many would say lack of planning) of the 1970s. High-rise hotels and apartment buildings now screen off the sea front and long golden beach, although two decades have mellowed their appearance.

In spite of Quarteira's aesthetic failings, a genuine Portuguese air prevails at the Vilamoura end of the beach, where a few seamen's shanty shacks still survive and where on Wednesdays the liveliest market in the Algarve is staged. There are some good inexpensive fish restaurants here, too. Quarteira's beach stretches all the way to the marina at Vilamoura.

Vilamoura to Oura

Vilamoura's huge **marina** is dominated by the futuristic lines of the 5-star Marinotel, which stares down on the seemingly endless rows of rich men's playthings. With berthing for over 600 craft, this is the biggest marina in the Algarve.

It's best at night when the quayside cafés and restaurants open up – by day it can be empty and soulless. Relief is provided, however, by the colourful, battered boats of the Vilamoura fishing fleet which constantly chug into and out of the harbour, providing a welcome contrast to the sleek white motor yachts which glide almost silently by. Like its affluent neighbours to the east, Vilamoura

The beach at Vale do Lobo.

provides some excellent sporting facilities.

The stark newness of Vilamoura's appearance belies the fact that it was originally a Roman dock. Some scant remains of the settlement, known as **Cerro da Vila**, may be seen, together with a small museum in the warden's house displaying finds from the site.

Beachlovers should also note that the dramatic red-ochre cliffs, which launched a thousand travel posters and set the Algarve on its way to international stardom, begin at Vilamoura's **Praia da Falésia**.

Olhos de Água means 'eyes of water', and this attractive small resort takes its name from eroded rocks (only visible at low tide) through which the seawater flows. A narrow road leads to a pretty beach which sunbathers share with the fishing fleet; behind is low-rise development. It can get very crowded in high season but otherwise has a relaxed atmosphere. There are two other very attractive beaches just along the coast, at **Balaia** and **Santa Eulália**, though these too may be busy in the high season with the overspill from Oura.

Not very long ago **Oura** was a quiet fishing village, quite separate from Albufeira which lies 3km (2 miles) to the west. Nowadays, the latter has spread its tentacles so much that in many a holiday brochure the two places are classified as one and the same, and a rash of little white boxes has filled every bit of space in between. The beach of **Praia da Oura** is still beautiful (if you can squeeze in). Adjoining the beach is the infamous 'Strip' – a bustling avenue of 'fun pubs', inexpensive restaurants and tacky bars which connects Praia da Oura with the resort of Montechoro.

Albufeira

The undisputed holiday capital of the Algarve, Albufeira has seen dramatic changes over the last two to three decades as it has evolved into a Mediterranean-style, mass-market super resort. Its best feature is its magnificent natural position, perched on enormous pock-marked sandstone cliffs which rise above two picture-book beaches, over which there are splendid **views**. The largest of these is the **Praia dos Barcos**

Albufeira is perched high on the cliffs overlooking the beaches.

The pretty old town of Albufeira is a network of steep, cobbled alleyways with whitewashed houses.

(Fishermen's Beach), and although the beach is still littered with traditional fishing boats, nowadays throngs of bronzing bodies wedge between their hulls, seeking shelter from the midday sun. The adjacent town bathing beach is equally crowded in summer.

The random, whitewashed Moorish **old town** of steep narrow streets has now been largely colonised by tourist shops, restaurants and bars, and only a small undeveloped area still survives. To see it, climb the steps next to the popular fish restaurant, **A Ruina** ('the ruins'), by the old fishmarket on the sea front. The ruins are those of the town's ancient Moorish castle, destroyed in the Great Earthquake of 1755 and now incorporated into the restaurant

41

The balmy Mediterranean evenings make dining under the stars a delight.

building. The Moors also gave Albufeira its name – derived from *Al-Buhera*, Arabic for 'castle-on-the-sea'. This was once an impregnable place, and as you wind up the tiring narrow streets it is easy to see why Albufeira was one of the last towns to fall during the Portuguese Reconquest.

At the top of the hill, the streets of Rua Nova, Rua da Igreja Velha, Rua do Cemitério Velho and Rua Henrique Calado are the remnants of unspoiled ancient Albufeira. This vantage point offers splendid views down to the town beach.

Another of Albufeira's few concessions to the past is to be found in the **Museu de Arte Sacra** (Museum of Sacred Art), housed in

he former **Igreja de São Sebastião** (Church
of St Sebastian). The church was built in the
18C, and includes a fine Manueline portal.
t also features a splendid gilt-painted carved
high altar in the classic Baroque style,
paintings and statuary salvaged from other
Algarve churches.

A few yards away, back towards the centre
of town (on Rua João de Deus), there is
another fascinating repository of ancient
fittings and furnishings at **A Tralha**, a
splendid antique shop, set in a beautiful old
house, which could easily be mistaken for a
museum.

The heart of town is the pedestrianised
square of **Largo E Duarte Pacheco**. Just
follow the cacophony of international voices
and music, and the chaotic mix of fashions
and food aromas which fill the surrounding
streets. In the evenings these are lined with
illuminated market stalls selling tourist
goods. As long as you do not mind crowds
and are not in search of the real Portugal,
it's all very jolly.

Albufeira also boasts two worthwhile
daytime markets: the colourful daily
fishmarket, also selling fruit, vegetables and
flowers (on the by-pass to Oura, closed
Monday), and the weekly **Gipsy Market** of
bric-a-brac, held at Cerro Grande (on the
way to Armação de Pêra) on the first and
third Tuesday of the month. You can also see
the fish being auctioned early each morning
on the Fishermen's Beach.

To escape most of the sunbathing crowds,
head immediately west of town to the
excellent beaches of **São Rafael**, **Coelha** and
Castelo. These are every bit as good as the
more popular sands to the east and are quiet
by comparison.

Armação de Pêra

If you are approaching **Armação de Pêra** from the west, try not to be put off by the initial impression of a high-rise building site and instead make your way to the pleasant promenade. The reward is one of the finest beaches in the Algarve. To the east, this stretches for miles – in fact almost all the way back to Albufeira – and here, too, the fishing fleet hauls up on the beach.

Directly below the promenade is the main section of the town beach, where, even in high season, there is plenty of room for

The beach of Armação de Pêra continues into the distance.

veryone. To the west are some impressive
roded rock formations. Boat trips from the
astern beach will take you past these
trangely sculpted rocks to 18 spectacular
ea caves.

There is little of cultural or historic
nterest (aside from a tiny 18C chapel) to
livert you from sunbathing. Vestiges of the
ld village may just be discerned in the
ackstreets to the east, but elsewhere the
own is devoted completely to shopping and
unning.

There is another beautiful beach 2km
1 mile) along the coast at **Senhora da
Rocha**. The *rocha* (rock) is a promontory

*The Capela de
Nossa Senhora da
Rocha enjoys
spectacular views
from the end of a
long headland.*

which juts for around 100m (329ft) into the
sea and rises sheer, enclosing a perfectly
protected bay. A scattering of fishing boats
completes the picture-postcard scene. At the
end of the rock is a small hexagonal-roofed
fishermen's chapel, **Capela de Nossa
Senhora da Rocha**, which enjoys panoramic
sea views. The interior is covered with
azulejos, and has interesting votive offerings
in the form of ships. A tunnel leads right
through the rock to another pretty beach.

Along the N 125

If you drive from Albufeira west in summer
you will almost certainly get stuck at the
traffic lights at **Alcantarilha**. It looks a
picturesque spot from the main road but
does not really live up to its promise at close
quarters.

However, tucked away in a side street by
the church there is a macabre **Capela dos
Ossos** (Chapel of Bones), containing the
skulls and bones of a thousand long-
departed parishioners (very similar to the
chapel at the Igreja do Carmo, Faro). It's a
fascinating but eerie place, especially so
when you learn that this was the only part of
the church to have survived the Great
Earthquake of 1755.

Rejoin the main road and any sombre
thoughts will soon be dispelled by the sight
of two of the Algarve's principal family
attractions, **The Big One** water park and
ZooMarine marine life and parrot park
(*see* p.108-109).

Porches is the centre of the Algarve's
pottery industry, and on the main road are
two very good outlets where you can buy
anything, from a miniature pottery rooster
to a complete set of antique *azulejos*. Porches

The Capela dos Ossos, at the Carmelite Church in Alcantarilha, withstood the Great Earthquake, while the rest of the church and buildings around it fell.

self is a small village just off the road, and is worth a detour. Look out for the private house with a superb example of a large filigreed Algarve chimney.

Lagoa (not to be confused with Lagos, to the west) is famous throughout the region for its wine, and you may even catch the aroma of fermenting grapes from the main road as you drive along. At harvest time

Terracotta pots on sale at Porches.

(late September/early October) wine lovers should seek out the Lagoa Co-operative, on the Portimão road, which showcases local produce.

Carvoeiro and its Beaches

A single road follows the long gully down from Lagoa to Carvoeiro, and eventually opens out onto a small beach, hemmed in by steep cliffs. **Carvoeiro** is a very pretty place, with many traditional buildings clinging to the hillsides, and lots of floral colour, but in recent years it has seen the arrival of blocks of white, low-rise (short-term rental) apartments.

To escape the commercialism, take the narrow roads to the beaches of **Vale de Centianes**, **Praia do Carvalho** and **Praia de**

enagil. The latter is particularly beautiful, ough recent road 'improvements' reaten the tranquillity of all three.

En route is **Algar Seco** (literally 'dry lley'), a cliffside hollowed and battered by nd and waves into beautiful rock ambers, grottoes, stone arches and range shapes. Steps descend to a lagoon closed within the rocks, and when the aves are calm this is a superb spot for orkelling. Beware, though, that at other mes you may risk being dashed against the cks. During the summer, the sea caves can e visited by boat.

The coastline around Carvoeiro, with its ochre cliffs, carved into weird shapes and grottoes, has numerous secluded coves, such as this one at Praia do Carvalho.

One of the many caves gouged in the rocks of Algar Seco by the pounding waves.

PRAIA DA ROCHA TO CAPE ST VINCENT

This section of the Algarve begins in some style, with a splendid new suspension bridge which seems to go on and on for ever, crossing the River Arade. The finale is equally impressive – the huge cliffs of **Cape St Vincent** (Cabo de São Vicente) was once thought to be *O Fim do Mundo* (Land's End). Henry the Navigator is reputed to have lived on the headland, where the lighthouse is now situated – it has the strongest beam in Europe, a suitable tribute to the nautically-minded prince. In between, around Praia da Rocha and Lagos, are some of the most beautiful beaches in Europe.

Portimão

Portimão, the 'Sardine Capital of the World', is changing. Until the very recent

ardines grilling in ortimão.

construction of the suspension bridge, your first impression of the town would probably have been gained sitting in a traffic jam, stuck on the road bridge above the barbecuing aromas of the **sardine dock**, where tourists feast daily on some of the best cheap lunches in the Algarve. Now it's easy to bypass the town altogether and head straight to the resorts. This would be a pity, however, as the sardine dock is well worth a visit. Take any one of the numerous river and sea **cruises** on offer at Portimão dock, and you will pass the fleet on your left hand side. Choose a cruise that goes east in order to see the splendid coastline around Carvoeiro, and particularly Algar Seco, (*see* p.49) from the seaward side.

Portimão also has a reputation as a shopping centre, and the main thoroughfares are Rua Vasco da Gama, Rua do Comércio, Rua Santa Isabel and Rua 5 de Outubro. If you're not shopping, make your first stop the charming Largo 1° de

This bench on Largo 1° Dezembro is one of ten in the square which are decorated with azulejos depicting scenes from Portuguese history. This one depicts the Battle of Aljubarrota, in 1385 (see p.9).

Dezembro, a small green square where ten benches are covered in *azulejos* (tiles) which depict some of the most crucial events in Portuguese history. The tourist office is also to be found here.

Follow the Rua Pimenta or Rua 5 de Outubro to the centre of town, to find the handsome **Igreja Matriz** (parish church), rebuilt after the Great Earthquake, though its 14C portal still remains. Almost opposite, the old fishmarket has been converted into a gallery, which stages exhibitions of ontemporary local artists' work.

After your visit to Portimão, follow the
iver Arade to its mouth and you will find
ourself in Praia da Rocha.

raia da Rocha to Alvor

holiday terms, **Praia da Rocha** ('beach
f the rocks') is the grand dame of the
lgarve. It has changed dramatically since
he 1930s, 40s and 50s when it was an artists'

*Sunbathers
scattered among
the rock formations
on Praia da Rocha.*

colony, drawing sensitive souls from all over
Europe to marvel at its magnificent beach,
dotted with scores of soaring rock stacks,
arches and other curious weathered
formations. Today it is one of the most
popular and most developed resorts in the
Algarve, with all the amenities of modern
tourism. The vast beach, with its series of
creeks, is always busy.

The town's main historical attraction is
the **Forte de Santa Catarina** (St Catharine's
Fort), built in the early 16C as protection
against marauding Moors. Little now
survives, but it's a fine spot to visit in the lat

*Relax at the café at
St Catharine's Fort,
where you can
watch the boats
come into harbour.*

afternoon, when you can watch the fishing
fleet returning home. Directly across the
river is another fortress at **Ferragudo**.
Unfortunately, this rather impressive
building is not open to the public. Access to
Ferragudo is just across the suspension
bridge (signed to Estômbar) and it is well
worth a trip. There are two fine beaches and
a charming small town, where life goes on
largely oblivious to the tourist commotion
across the river.

The great long beach of Praia da Rocha
stretches on to become **Praia do Vau**, before
high-rise blocks mark the next major tourist
development at **Alvor**.

The small town of Alvor, about 1km

*The more relaxed
village of Ferragudo
lies across the
estuary from Praia
da Rocha.*

(0.5 mile) west of the long main beach, has been colonised by tourist restaurants and bars, but has managed to retain a good deal of its character. Narrow, whitewashed streets dive down to the quay and fishmarket, from where the lagoon and wetlands of the Alvor estuary form a picturesque scene. There are some good fish and seafood restaurants here, too. The 16C **Igreja Matriz** (parish church) is worth a look, for its fine

The towering rock formations of Praia do Vau still hold their own against the competing high-rise developments.

Manueline portal and its *azulejos* (*see* p.18).

There is no road across the Alvor estuary, so to continue west to Lagos you have to strike back inland to the EN 320.

Lagos

Your introduction to Lagos is the **Avenida dos Descobrimentos** (Avenue of the Discoveries), which runs along the river, separating town from port and marina. Towards the far end of the Avenue, in Praça da República, is a handsome **statue** of Prince Henry the Navigator, who made Lagos his headquarters. His palace is presumed to have stood just behind where the statue is now located, but sadly was lost forever in the Great Earthquake of 1755, together with all relics. His other base at Cabo São Vicente was also destroyed, and although his fort at Sagres is still there, it is in a very poor state. A vestige of one of the more unsavoury aspects of Portuguese maritime history remains, however. Look for the small arcade behind and to the right of the statue. A tiny plaque, engraved **Mercado de Escravos** (Slave Market), indicates that the first slaves in Europe were sold here from 1444 onwards.

War parties also used Lagos as a base. The last of these sailed from the beach of Meia Praia in 1578 under the inexperienced command of the boy-king, Dom Sebastião, for the doomed battle of El-Ksar El-Kebir, in Morocco (*see* p.12). A modern **statue** of Dom Sebastião (who was killed in the battle) stands on Praça Gil Eanes. This monument depicts the king as an androgynous, futuristic figure dressed in a silver foil-like suit and motorbike gauntlets.

For a more conventional interpretation of the town's history, visit the intriguing

...hibits in the ...useum in Lagos.

collection of the **Museu Regional de Lagos**
(Regional Museum), which includes
ecclesiastical treasures and some interesting
archaeological finds. Next door, the **Igreja
de Santo António** (Church of St Anthony)
contains some of the finest and most
ebullient gilt Baroque woodwork in the
country. Carved around 1715, it is a rare
survivor of the Great Earthquake.

*...e extravagant
...ded woodwork in
...e Church of St
...nthony, Lagos,
...ve rise to its
...her name, the
...olden Chapel.*

Also at this end of town is the **Forte da
Ponta da Bandeira** (literally 'fort at flag
point'), a smart little black-and-white sea
fort, built in the 17C, though it has been
much restored recently. It now contains a
small museum.

The charm of Lagos is best enjoyed by

simply wandering at will. In its quiet, cobbled backstreets life goes on more or le[ss] as it has for centuries. Walk in any directio[n] and before too long you will come to the ci[ty] walls. They are still mostly intact and date back to the 16C.

When you return to the main street of Rua 25 de Abril – touristy, though still attractive – do pay a visit to the fascinating Aladdin's Cave antique shop of **Casa do Papagaio**. There are also a number of trendy bars and some good restaurants in the area. For the best view of the city and it[s]

Fishing boats in front of the Forte da Ponta da Bandeira.

There are plenty of shops to browse in the narrow cobblestoned streets of Lagos.

walls, cross the river to the colourful fishing port.

Lagos's main attraction is, without doubt, its beaches. The long flat sands of **Meia Praia** stretch for some 4km (2.5 miles) to the east of town, while to the west are some of the most picturesque coves in the Algarve. The best of these are **Dona Ana** and **Praia do Camilo**, both flanked by huge red and ochre sandstone cliffs with amazing wind- and wave-formed grottoes and rock stacks.

Ponta da Piedade (Bridge of Pity) is a famous spectacular rock arch with grottoes which can be toured daily by fishing boat.

You can join one of these trips from Lagos, or walk down the vertiginous steps at Ponta da Piedade which descend to the sparkling aquamarine waters. There is no beach here but this a lovely spot for snorkelling. Ponta da Piedade is also a popular place to come in the evening to watch the sunset.

Ironically – with several hotels right on Meia Praia beach, and everyone else keen to decamp to the picture-postcard coves to the west – the pleasant small **town beach**, next to the fort, is usually relatively uncrowded.

The dramatic beauty of Ponta da Piedade makes it a popular spot to watch the sun go down.

*view to the beach
from the sandstone
cliffs at Dona Ana.*

Praia da Luz to Vila do Bispo

Praia da Luz, 9km (5.5 miles) west of Lagos,
is a popular spot, particularly with British
families, and has a quieter, less cosmopolitan
atmosphere than Lagos. It features an
excellent crescent-shaped beach, bordered
by huge flat rocks where many visitors lap up
the sun like lizards. There are good
watersports facilities here, and most
accommodation is to be found in villas.
There is not a lot to see in old Luz itself, the
main historical attraction being its fort, now
converted into a restaurant.

Just west, **Burgau** is less developed than Luz, with fewer facilities and a less attractive beach. Yet this small fishing village has retained much of its character. Boats are pulled up onto the small beach, and even onto the hillside road.

Salema is the final developed resort heading west. A number of fishermen still sail from here. It boasts a fine, long, sandy beach, and its steep, narrow, cobbled streets retain a good deal of its original character. Holiday developments are growing apace, and now almost fill the valley behind the resort.

The pretty beach at Luz offers good watersports, and a relaxed and peaceful atmosphere.

*he charming
shing village of
urgau makes a
efreshing
ternative to some
f the more
eveloped resorts
long the Algarve.*

If you want to escape the crowds and
building developments altogether, continue
west, then head north at Vila do Bispo to the
wild beaches of the west coast. Note though
that the water is colder and rougher than on
the south coast, and there are few facilities
of any kind. Some of the beaches further
north are popular with New Age types. **Vila
do Bispo** merits a stop for its pretty Baroque
church. Built in the 18C, it features some
excellent *azulejos*, and its ceiling is covered
with frescoes.

Sagres

Ponta de Sagres stars in just about every travel agent's itinerary, and the famous **fortress of Henry the Navigator** is presented almost as a place of romantic pilgrimage. The reality is more prosaic. In fact, 500 years ago this must have been a shadowy, forbidding place, akin to modern-day, high-tech, high security government establishments such as Aldermaston in the UK or Los Alamos in the US. The approach to the fortress is still daunting – its great grey bulk seems almost to fill the horizon as you roll towards it on an arrow-straight entrance road.

No-one knows quite what went on here. Those parts that survived the violent attentions of Sir Francis Drake in 1587 (who tragically burned Henry's Library) were all but destroyed by the Great Earthquake. Sadly, recent restoration of the fort has disfigured the last vestiges of the age and character of the site. Inside the courtyard of the fortress is a small 16C chapel. There is also a small museum. Most experts agree that one of the original functions of this institution was as an observation point. The most obvious indication of this is the huge **rosa dos ventos** (stone rose compass) still clearly visible on the floor, measuring 43m (141ft) across. Above it (climb the steps) is a small sundial.

It is believed that here at Ponta de Sagres, Prince Henry the Navigator gathered the greatest minds of the day – astronomers, astrologers, geographers, cartographers, mariners and shipbuilders – in order to launch his far-flung expeditions. Today the traffic has reversed, and visitors from every corner of the globe travel here, while the

The enormous stone rose compass hints at past activities at the Ponta de Sagres.

most daring exploits are those of local fishermen who perch precariously on the cliff-edge, with their extra long rods and lines dangling some 60m (180ft) down into the foaming waters.

The town of **Sagres** is enlivened by a mix of young international travellers. At the centre is the small square of **Praça da República**, where there are cafés, restaurants and a privately run tourist office. The port and several good beaches are close at hand. Perhaps the best is **Praia do Martinhal**, very popular with windsurfers.

Sagres claims one of the Algarve's most prestigious hotels, the **Pousada do Infante**, one of only two state-run hotels in the region (*see* p.93). The *pousada* is completely modern, but as you head towards the very tip of the Algarve, do stop at the charming small **Fortaleza do Beliche**. This little white fortress was built in the 17C, and now

is easy to see why ople thought the amatic headland Cabo de São cente lay at the ge of the world.

functions as a restaurant and as an annexe to the Pousada do Infante.

Cabo de São Vicente

Some 6km (4 miles) from Sagres is Europe's most south-westerly point, Cabo de São Vicente (Cape St Vincent). Before the voyages of Henry, this point was regarded as *O Fim do Mundo* – Land's End. Beyond were sea serpents, boiling seas and incertitude. Even today, as you stare out into the great blue expanse of the Atlantic Ocean, such thoughts can be easily conjured.

The cape is still an important shipping landmark and the lighthouse (rarely open to the public) is home to Europe's most powerful lamp, visible from up to 90km (55 miles) away.

Birdwatchers and botanists will enjoy this area, particularly in spring. But no visitor can fail to be impressed by the awe-inspiring scale and forlorn grandeur of the place. It's nearly always blustery here, so pack a sweater.

EXPLORING THE COUNTRYSIDE

Despite the stereotype, a good number of visitors do stir from their beach towels and venture inland, and are richly rewarded for their efforts. If you time your visit to avoid the tourist buses, and wine and dine away from the obvious gathering points, you can still find the old Algarve.

CENTRAL ALGARVE HINTERLAND

Saturday is the best day to tour this area, as this coincides with the Loulé market. However, this also means you will find a fair number of fellow tourists, so the best advice is to start early, before the tourist buses.

If you are staying to the east of Loulé, the route below is best followed clockwise, as listed, but those staying west of Paderne should take a counter-clockwise direction.

Loulé

Loulé is famous throughout the region, primarily for its Saturday market. In fact, there are two markets each Saturday. You'll find most of the locals at the boisterous **food market**, set in and around the atmospheric mock-Moorish market halls, right in the centre of town. Noisy stallholders preside over buckets of olives and boxes of chicks, and old women swathed in black sit outside selling bunches of herbs and vegetables. The so-called **Gipsy Market** takes place about 100m (300ft) away, just off the town's main boulevard, which on Saturdays is chock-a-

The food market at Loulé is where locals shop.

Moorish-style pottery on sale at the Gipsy Market.

...ock with pavement cafés. Gipsies do indeed flock here to sell everyday items, odds and ends and tourist trinkets, but many of the tourist wares are on sale throughout the coastal resorts. Still, don't let that put you off; it's a colourful and lively occasion and you can find some genuine craft items.

Loulé is not just a market town. It is well known as a **craft centre** in its own right, and gathered around the castle ruins are a

number of shops and studios where you can watch artisans making furniture and pottery, beating copper and brass, and working leather. Like many of the town's crafts, the **castle** dates from Moorish times. It is well worth the short climb up the ramparts to look over the unspoilt Loulé roofscape. Also within the castle confines is the tourist office and a small museum of local items. Opposite is the **Igreja da Nossa Senhora da Conceição** (Church of Our Lady of the Conception), its plain exterior belying a beautiful interior of gilt woodwork and blue-and-white *azulejos*. If it is closed, you can usually get the key from no 27, or ask at the tourist office.

The town's third claim to fame is its **Carnival** celebrations, which are the best in the region (*see* p.91).

As you leave Loulé in the direction of Salir, you will see straight ahead of you a curious large, truncated, Classical column. This is, in fact, a monument dedicated to Duarte Pacheco, a Minister of Public Works, who died in 1943.

Salir

Salir, 16km (10 miles) north of Loulé, is a charming small hamlet which is off the main tourist trail and sits on two hills joined by a steep ridge. The newer part clusters around a large church, which dates back to the 16C, and an even larger water tower. The best view of 'new Salir' is to be had from the adjacent hill, signposted **Castelo do Mouro** (The Moor's Castle). All that remains of what must once have been a redoubtable stronghold are the bases of its four large corner turrets. Scattered around the castle ruins are picturesque white houses and a friendly *miradouro* (lookout point) café.

The picturesque village of Salir nestles among the tree-clad hills.

Alte

Follow the road west for 13km (8 miles) to Alte, the Algarve's most picturesque and best-known village. Before entering the village, follow the signs to **Fonte Grande** and **Fonte Pequena**. Go past the Fonte Pequena restaurant, a very popular folk-dancing venue, towards the source of the *fonte* (springs) where at weekends children splash around in the cool, clear water. The colourful May Day celebrations finish with a procession to the stream.

Alongside is a café and a picnic/barbecue area, packed with locals whose grilling food turns the air thick with aromatic clouds, particularly on Sundays. It's an excellent place for refreshments and cooling off, particularly if you have children.

The village itself lies across a small white bridge crossing a babbling river. At the centre is the beautiful 15C **Igreja Matriz** (parish church) with *azulejos* from Seville. Guided tours point out the various national saints to which the church's many side altars are dedicated. Note, too, the superb Manueline portal at the front entrance. The rest of the village, full of whitewashed picture-postcard houses, with doors and windows painted in primary colours, and walls splashed with bougainvillaea, is well worth exploring.

One of the altars of the Igreja Matriz (parish church) in Alte.

The pretty village of Alte was awarded second most picturesque village in a national competition in the 1930s; despite tourism, it still retains its appeal.

Paderne

This attractive village lies off the main tourist track. Its Moorish **castle** stands well to the south of the village, by Fonte de Paderne. Inside the castle walls are the vestiges of a Gothic chapel. In Paderne itself are some fine old buildings and the 16C **Igreja Matriz** (parish church).

If you start your tour at Paderne and are heading east to Loulé, be alert for a bizarre but well-documented phenomenon. East of Boliqueime, by the Eurocampina factory, there is a hill which seems to defy the laws of gravity. Cars roll backwards *up* the hill! Test it by stopping, then releasing your hand brake (making sure the road is clear of traffic first, of course). If the force is with you, your car will roll up the hill, and can attain quite some speed! Is it a magnetic force (some say released by local quarrying), an optical illusion, or just a modern myth?

WESTERN ALGARVE HINTERLAND

This area is dominated by the **Serra de Monchique**, a range of brooding volcanic hills which rise to over 900m (nearly 3 000ft). There are fine views of the area, and the densely wooded hills offer a refreshing retreat from the hot coast. Below the hills lies Silves, the Algarve's most impressive historic town.

Silves: Rise and Fall

Silves is situated some 16km (10 miles) upstream of Portimão, on the River Arade, once an important highway. The city's origins date back to the Romans and beyond, as may be discovered in the modern archaeological museum. It was under the

The ruins of the castle at Silves, set high on a hill, dominate the town.

Arabs, however, that Chelb (or Xelb) as it was then called, reached its zenith. Between the 8C and the 12C, its population rose to over 30 000 and the town became an important centre of culture and commerce (*see* p.9). Lemons, oranges and cork were the chief commodities loaded here and shipped down the Arade.

The Arab cistern of Silves now forms the centrepiece of the Municipal and Archaeological Museum.

Contemporary historians compared the beauty of the city to Baghdad, and describe Chelb as being far more powerful than Lisbon. With the construction of its splendid red castle there are even comparisons to be drawn with Spain's famous Alhambra.

True to those troubled times, however, Silves was no stranger to violence. One of the many legends surrounding the town concerns the macabre humour of one of its rulers, Al-Mu'tadid of Seville: he is suppose to have used the painted skulls of his decapitated enemies as flower pots to decorate the palace gardens. Nemesis came in 1189 in the form of King Dom Sancho, who enlisted the services of Crusaders and

besieged the castle for several months. When at last Chelb surrendered, the Crusaders ignored the terms of the treaty and the wishes of Dom Sancho. They ransacked the town, killing some 6 000 Moors and torturing others into revealing where their treasures were hidden. The city was retaken by the Moors in 1191, but was lost forever in the final Reconquest in 1242. Over time the Arade silted up, and with the loss of Moorish wealth and skills the city declined to become a deserted backwater. By the late 16C, its population had declined to a mere 140.

*quiet
cobblestoned
backstreet in Silves.*

Silves Today

Although the current town population is
around 10 000, Silves still has a very sleepy
atmosphere, with the Arade flowing lazily
past the city walls and beneath a four-arched
bridge which dates back to Roman times. In
an enterprising new tourism venture, flat-
bottomed boats make the trip up the river
from Portimão. Silves is also still famous for
its citrus groves which, together with
farming and tourism, have restored a degree
of prosperity.

The crowning glory of the town is the
beautifully restored **castle**, which offers
sweeping views from its ramparts. Ironically,
the only monument in the castle grounds
commemorates the man responsible for its
demise, Dom Sancho, lionised by a
forbidding larger-than-life statue. Even
more ironically for a fortress that was
originally built by Muslims, the high point of
the Silves annual events calendar is a beer
festival, held inside the castle walls each July
(*see* p.92).

Adjacent to the castle is the **Sé**
(cathedral), an imposing, largely Gothic
building. The tombs within are thought to
belong to those Crusaders who helped
finally capture the city in 1242. Nearby is the
Museu Municipal de Arqueologia
(Municipal and Archaeological Museum),
built around a large Arab water cistern, and
the **Torreão das Portas da Cidade** (city gate
tower), a powerful, well-preserved barbican.

Most organised excursions combine Silves
with Caldas de Monchique, Monchique and
Fóia. For a quieter day, with less mileage,
you could combine Silves with a visit to the
Barragem do Arade, a scenic reservoir 6km
(4 miles) to the north-east. Here, in

Beautiful ceramics like these on sale in Monchique can be found all over the Algarve.

summer, there is a restaurant and watersport facilities. En route, just outside Silves, is the **Cruz de Portugal** (Portuguese Cross), a weather-beaten 16C statue depicting the Crucifixion on one side and the Descent from the Cross on the other.

The volcanic landscape around Caldas de Monchique has given rise to the medicinal springs found here.

Caldas de Monchique

The road north to Caldas de Monchique is one of the most picturesque in the Algarve, ascending steeply through lush forests of chestnut, cork-oak, pine and eucalyptus.

Like Silves, Caldas de Monchique (literally, 'the spa of Monchique') dates back to Roman times. Today, it seems firmly locked in an Edwardian time warp, with a collection of elegant 19C and early 20C buildings set in a picturesque leafy valley with a bubbling stream. The main building in the square, with coloured glass windows, used to be a gambling casino, a reminder of its mid 19C heyday, when Caldas de Monchique was a fashionable resort.

It's a tiny spot whose atmosphere can rapidly evaporate with the arrival of tourist buses, so it is important to come here early (before 10am), or late. If you do make it early, you can watch a local speciality, *pão com chouriço* (spicy sausage in a bread roll), being baked in a traditional outdoor kiln, next to the rustic restaurant, **O Tasco**.

The waters of Caldas de Monchique have been famous for many centuries, and King Dom João II was a notable visitor in 1495. You can try it free, fresh from the source, or drink the rather more palatable bottled version available all over the Algarve. There are many long-term visitors who stay here to take the waters and to benefit from the various forms of hydrotherapy offered.

Just above the spa is a *miradouro* (lookout point) offering an excellent view down to the coast. Before you continue north to Monchique it's worth detouring as far as **Marmelete** (14km/9 miles east of the main Monchique) for more fine **views** of the Serra de Monchique. Aljezur, with its Moorish ruins and beautiful setting, is the next town of interest (*see* p.86), 15km (9.5 miles) further west.

Monchique and Fóia

The village of **Monchique** has long been known as a handicraft centre and although in recent years it has expanded considerably, it has managed to retain much of its charm. Here you will find craftsmen making the distinctive pottery of the Algarve, shoemakers, and basket-makers (who practise the ancient craft of pollarding locally grown willows to provide the flexible shoots needed for the baskets).

Monchique is also famous for its **Igreja Matriz** (parish church), which boasts a much-photographed Manueline porch. The church interior is notable for its wooden ceiling and pretty *azulejos*.

From Monchique, a road strikes west for 8km (5 miles) ending at **Pico da Fóia**. At an altitude of 902m (2 959ft), this is the highest spot not only in the Serra de Monchique, but in all the Algarve. On a clear day you can see all the way to Cape St Vincent, and (according to the poet Robert Southey) even as far as Sintra.

The number of souvenir and handicraft stalls testify to the fact that Fóia caters primarily to the tourist trade, but the chunky woollens on sale (to protect against the cold wind) can be excellent value.

*e Manueline
rtal of the parish
urch has
teresting twisted
ope' columns,
otted at intervals
und the doorway.*

GAZETTEER
The best of the rest – see them
if you have time, or perhaps as
a change from the more visited
towns and villages of the
Algarve.

Aljezur
Sited roughly half-way up the
west coast, Aljezur makes a
good base for exploring the
beaches of Arrifana, Amoreira
and Monte Clérigo, and is also
the terminus of the pic-
turesque road that travels east-
west through the Serra de
Monchique. There are old and
new parts to the town, but you
should forget the latter and
cross the bridge to the historic
town, nestled under a ruined
Moorish castle.

Monte Clérigo, north-west of Aljezur.

The Barragem da Bravura.

Barragem da Bravura

The fertile countryside around this picturesque semi-natural *barragem* (reservoir) lake is typical of the Algarve agricultural hinterland, abundant with orange and lemon groves. The lake itself is a welcome and unusual sight in such a parched region, though it is not easily accessible for swimming or other water activities.

Fuseta

A nascent resort, patronised by more adventurous travellers, Fuseta lies half-way between Olhão and Tavira, on a creek with a small fishing fleet and working salt pans. Its beach is a short boat ride away, on the eastern tip of the Ilha da Armona.

Moncarapacho

Just north of Olhão and east of Estói, the hills of Moncarapacho, lush with orange and almonds groves, are excellent for walking.

There are also limestone

caves (*grutas*) to be explored, and wonderful views down to the coast from Monte de São Miguel.

In the middle of the sleepy village is the handsome Gothic church of Santo Cristo, with some fine polychromatic 18C *azulejos*. Adjacent is an interesting small museum featuring sacred art, archaeology and curiosities.

São Brás de Alportel

For six days of the week the main attraction of this typical dusty rural crossroads town (just east of Loulé) is its charming **Museu Etnográfico do Trajo Algarvio** (Museum of Algarve Costume). On a Saturday, however, São Brás comes to life with a bustling fresh produce market.

Just south of town, enjoying a fine hillside situation, is the Pousada de São Brás de Alportel, a somewhat spartan representative of the Portuguese state-run hotel chain.

The busy produce market at São Brás de Alportel.

WEATHER

The Algarve climate is Mediterranean: warm all year round, with extremes of temperature rare. Its popularity lies in its 300 days of sunshine annually. High season is July and August, when midday land temperatures soar as high as 30°C (86°F). A dip in the sea will cool you off more than you bargained for, however. It is easy to forget that this is the Atlantic, which is several degrees cooler than the Mediterranean. Winters are usually comfortably warm, with temperatures often around 17°C (62°F), though it can get quite chilly in the evenings. There are a few rainy days between October and March.

In such a small area there are no real climatic differences, but even in the summer you may need a sweater for the highest points of the Serra de Monchique and for the windy westernmost points of Sagres and Cabo de São Vicente. You will also notice strong Atlantic winds if you explore the beaches of the west coast, where the sea is even cooler than that off the south coast. You should also be prepared for the Atlantic waves, especially if you have children.

CALENDAR OF EVENTS

In addition to the events listed below, each town and village celebrates its particular patron saint's day with processions, fireworks and other festivities. Consult the local tourist office for other events and also ask them for a copy of their monthly events brochure.

January
Between New Year and Twelfth Night:
Charolas (carols) are performed by wandering troupes all over the Algarve.

*this colourful
stival, the lady of
e house carries
owers on her head
representing local
ats of arms.*

February

The long weekend before Lent: Carnival, including the Battle of the Flowers, at Loulé is the biggest pre-Lent festival in the Algarve, with processions, elaborately decorated floats and grand firework displays.

March/April

Easter Sunday: Loulé is also the venue for the Romaria da Nossa Senhora da Piedade (Our Lady of Pity). The centre of this festival involves the carrying of a 16C effigy of the Virgin Mary into the town from a shrine in nearby Monte da Piedade, whence it returns after a short stay at the Igreja Matriz (parish church). Processions are also held throughout the province, notably in Faro.

May

May Day: Celebrations and folk festivals are held throughout the Algarve on this public holiday. The most famous one, at Alte, culminates in a procession to the springs. Celebrations continue into 2 and 3 May at Estói, as May Day merges into the Estói Festa da Pinha (Pine Festival).
Second week of May: Salir is a charming setting for the Festa da Espiga (Grain Festival), with floats, fireworks and folk dancing.
Film buffs should note that Praia da Rocha hosts the Algarve Film Festival in May.

June

1 June: The Festival Internacional de Música do Algarve (Algarve Music Festival) runs for six weeks, with a series of concerts and ballets staged throughout the region by local, national and international performers.

Last week of the month: The Festejos dos Santos Populares (Feast of the Popular Saints) is held at Tavira. This century-old tradition features music, dancing and regional foods.

July
Around 16 July: The Feira da Nossa Senhora do Carmo in Faro is a traditional fair, featuring local arts and crafts.
End of the month: Silves Castle is the surprising venue for the very popular Festival da Cerveja (Beer Festival): two weeks of quaffing beers from around the world, accompanied by brass bands and folk dancing.

August
Middle of the month: The Festival do Marisco (Seafood Festival) is at Olhão.
15 August: Feast of the Assumption at Castro Marim.
FATACIL (Feira de Artesanato, Turismo, Agricultura, Comércio e Indústria de Lagoa): This is nominally a trade fair, but is open to the public and is a good opportunity to see the best of the Algarve's handicrafts.

September
Around mid-month: The colourful Festival Nacional de Folclore (Folk Music and Dance Festival) is held throughout the region, over four days. On the last day, a competition is held on the beach at Praia da Rocha, involving groups from all over Portugal.

October
26 to 28 October: Monchique hosts an important country fair.

ACCOMMODATION

The *Michelin Red Guide Portugal* contains information on accommodation available in the Algarve. The region offers several types of accommodation, ranging from the most luxurious of establishments to the most modest pension.

Pousadas are state-run hotels, the equivalent of Spain's *paradores*. They are either purpose-built hotels or restored historic buildings, and all have at least one outstanding feature: either a particularly beautiful setting or sumptuous furnishings and top-class service. There are only two in the Algarve (with 30 throughout Portugal) so early booking is essential (*see* p.68). More

e modern Hotel Paz, at Praia da ocha, reflects the oorish influence.

information can be obtained from
ENATUR, Avenida Santa Joana Princesa 10,
1700 Lisboa ☎ (01) 848 1221. *Estalgens*
provide similar accommodation, but these
are privately owned establishments.

Hotels are graded from one up to five
stars and the Portuguese Tourist Board
publishes listings of these. Facilities become
more extensive with the increase in stars, but
even one-star hotels are clean and efficient.
Taxes and breakfast are nearly always
included in the price given, but it is as well
to check. A rough guide to prices, per
double room per night, is given below (but
remember that prices are not regulated and
are not necessarily related to star ratings):

One-star: 6 000 escudos
Two-star: 9 000 escudos
Three-star: 12 000 escudos
Four-star: 15 000 escudos
Five-star: 25 000 escudos or more

Residencias and *Pensões* are guesthouses;
similar to some hotels in terms of facilities,
they often do not serve meals.

Bed and breakfast accommodation is also
available in traditional, often rather
handsome, Portuguese houses under the
Turismo de Habitação (TH) scheme. For
more rural accommodation, apply to the
Associação de Casas de Turismo (ACT), Alto
de Pampilheira Torre de 8°A, 2750 Cascais
☎ (01) 484 4464.

For families, self-catering complexes are a
popular option. Alternatively, private rooms
and flats can be rented; ask at the local
tourist office about both.

There are 18 youth hostels in Portugal,
open to holders of a YHA International
Card. For further information contact the
Associação Portuguesa das Pousadas de

ventude Avenida Duque de Ávila 137,
00 Lisboa ☎ (01) 355 9081.

ere are a few **recommendations** (unless
herwise specified, the following hotels
arge from 8 500 to 12 000 escudos for a
uble room):

bufeira: Vila Galé Praia (Albufeira;
089 59 10 50) Situated in the residential
ea, Praia da Galé, behind the beach.
ro: Ibis Faro (Pontes de Marchil
089 80 67 71) A good stop-over at a
asonable price.
rk (Rua de Berlim 39; ☎ 089 82 39 73)
all villa situated in the residential area.
gos: Marazul (Rua 25 de Abril 13;
082 76 91 43) Excellent family-run
ablishment.
ves: Quinta do Rio, Country Inn (Rua São
tévão; ☎ 082 44 55 28) Small rural inn
tside Silves, amidst orange groves.
vira: Convento de Santo Antonio
talaia 56; ☎ 081 32 56 32) A charming
all hotel in reconverted monastery with
isters (20 000 escudos).

OOD AND DRINK

ach of the Algarve's cuisine is derived
m the basic dishes of fishermen and
asants. At its simplest, this can mean a
nu of vegetable soup and grilled sardines.
more elaborate dishes, pork and shellfish
e often combined, and in others the
luence of the Portuguese colonies is very
dent.
Fresh **fish and shellfish** are the speciality
the Algarve. A favourite meal consists of
ge, plump, crisply grilled *sardinhas*
rdines), served in the traditional way with
ad and boiled potatoes.
Bife de atum is a meaty tuna steak fillet,

A typical Algarvian lunch.

marinated and cooked with onion. *Espada* (or *peixe agulha*) is swordfish, also often served as a steak. Don't confuse this with *peixe espada*, the long thin black or silver fi which yield a sweet white flesh. The most famous and enterprising Portuguese shellfish dish is *cataplana* (seafood, sausag ham, onion, garlic and paprika), named after the hinged, wok-like cooker in which is prepared and served. Other types of shellfish include *lavagante* (lobster with la front claws), *lagostim/lagosta* (spiny lobster/crayfish, without front claws), *sapateira* (a type of Atlantic crab) and *San* (spider crab). Unfortunately, these and other types of shellfish are now very expensive, but make a delicious treat.

The other ubiquitous fish dish is the Portuguese national favourite, *bacalhau* (pronounced, berk-el'-yow, the last syllable to rhyme with wow). Ironically, even though fresh fish is available on the doorstep all year round, *bacalhau* is dried, salted cod, first discovered on voyages to Newfoundland in the 14C, and ever since imported from northern waters. It bears a close resemblance to stiff yellow cardboard, and before cooking must be soaked repeatedly to wash away the salt. This type of preserving makes for a strong and pungent flavour, so most *bacalhau* is casseroled with other ingredients. There are dozens of *bacalhau* dishes; indeed, the Portuguese claim to have 365 different varieties – one for each day of the year.

The finest **meat** in Portugal is said to come from the Alentejo region on the northern border of the Algarve, where the little black pigs gorge themselves on acorns; wherever you go, you'll find excellent **pork** dishes. The most unusual combination is *porco com amêijoas/porco à alentejana* (marinated pork, cooked with cockles or clams). *Leitão* (suckling pig), served hot or cold, is another speciality. A tasty local starter is *presunto*, smoked ham, from the Serra de Monchique region.

Chicken (*frango*) is a staple dish, either simply roasted or barbecued, or marinated *piri-piri* style before cooking. Piri-piri are small hot red peppers from the former colony of Angola. The resultant dish is deliciously spicy, though rarely too hot for the average palate. The other exotic dish to appear on many a menu is curry, from Goa

(South India) or Africa.

In traditional restaurants and *tascas* (taverns), **soup** is always on the menu. Many broths are thickened with potatoes and served in such hearty portions that they could suffice as a main course. Soup with egg is a Portuguese peculiarity: *sopa à alentejana* and *açorda* are both garlic and bread soups, the former includes a poached egg, the latter a raw egg. If seafood is added, this becomes *açorda de marisco*. *Canja de galinha* is a chicken broth with rice and boiled eggs, while *sopa de cozido* is rich and meaty.

Vegetarians will soon gather that Algarvian cuisine is not geared towards their needs. Restaurants in large towns sometimes provide 'vegetarian' options, but be careful as 'bean stew' will often include fish, bacon and sausage. Vegetables are not used with

Sampling the local wines is an enjoyable element of any stay in the Algarve.

any great variety in the Algarve, and salads rarely constitute more than a garnish, but picnicking on fresh market produce and some of the delicious range of breads available might make an attractive option.

The Algarve has no world famous **table wines**, though the local brands, particularly from Lagoa and Tavira, are more than acceptable. A northern Portuguese speciality is *vinho verde* (literally 'green wine'). The name refers to its fresh, youthful, slightly sparkling nature and, well chilled, it is a perfect accompaniment to seafood.

The country's most famous drink, of course, is **port**. Although this is not an Algarve speciality, most visitors to the Algarve do wish to sample it, prompted no doubt by the fact that the shelves of wine shops and supermarkets are packed with its various types and a multitude of brands, all at prices well below those charged abroad. Here are a few helpful hints.

White port (often referred to as 'dry white') has a taste akin to a full-bodied medium-dry sherry, and makes a perfect aperitif. It should always be served chilled. **Tawny** (so called because of its light brown colour) has a slightly nutty taste and also makes a good aperitif. An Old Tawny is a richer, aged version of Tawny. **Vintage port** is the finest quality of all, with a rich, complex, fruity flavour, and is usually drunk after dinner. All port is regulated, but the strictest rules of all apply to what constitutes a vintage port. **Late-bottled vintage port** often makes a very good substitute, usually lighter on the palate and always lighter on the purse.

If you would like to sample a little Algarve moonshine, try *medronho*, the local firewater,

The street cafés are open during the evenings for drinks or meals.

distilled from the red berries of the arbutu. bush. *Bagaço* and *bagaceira* are equally potent, made (in the same fashion as *marc*, *grappa* etc.) from the detritus of the wine-making process.

Eating out is mostly casual in the Algarve reflecting its mass-market popularity, thoug there are some excellent top-class restaurants too. Those in search of an exceptional culinary experience should try the Vila Joya near Albufeira and the Ermitage and Sao Gabriel in Almancil. On the whole, however, prices are reasonable i most restaurants, though no longer very cheap by northern European standards. Many restaurants offer a three-course *emen turística* (tourist menu), which is the

heapest, though often the least inspiring,
ay to eat.

Beware though, portions are usually
enerous, and as you will be charged for the
apparently complimentary) olives/cream
heese/sardine spread which are brought to
ou before you order, you may not need any
ther starter.

Coffee is important in the Algarve, and
here are many **cafés** which serve speciality
offees and snacks. The licensing laws are
ery relaxed, and a bar is the focal point of
ost cafés. Plates of lupin seeds are often
laced on the bar for the patrons to nibble
ee of charge. *Pastelarias* (cake shops, also
cluding a bar) are another frequent sight.
ocals often stop off here for a coffee, a
lass of brandy and a sugary cake to start the
ay. The Algarvian tendency towards sweet
ings is said to have been inherited from
e Moors. The inclusion of almond paste in
ost cakes would seem to testify to this.

ecommendations

iscovering restaurants on your own is part
f the fun of any holiday, but here are a few
oderately-priced restaurants to get you
arted.

lmancil: Bistro des Z'Arts (French bistro)

aro: Cidade Velha (friendly restaurant in
e Old Town)

agos: Dom Sebastião (traditional rustic
tmosphere)

ortimão: Casa Real (excellent service,
mily-run)

agres: Fortaleza do Beliche (quietly
tuated in a fortress on the headland
verlooking the sea; rooms also available)

avira (Quatro Águas): Portas do Mar
specialises in fish and seafood, overlooking
e beach)

rolling around the ops in the destrianised eas of Lagos is a light.

SHOPPING

The Algarve is no longer the bargain basement of Iberia and, as with all mass-market tourist destinations, cheap Far Eastern products have infiltrated and displaced local craft items. **Markets** provide the most fun, and usually the best prices, particularly if you are prepared to haggle. Ask the tourist office for a list of local markets.

Metal-working is another Moorish legacy and may be seen first-hand in the back streets of Loulé, where you can buy an assortment of brass, bronze and copper goods. Liquor stills and *cataplana* (*see* p.96) cookers are two of the more attractive and unusual items often displayed in the kitchens of Algarve visitors.

There is a plethora of **leather goods**, particularly bags, to sort through, but remember you get what you pay for (ignore 'factory price' signs). Shoes are still good value and some of the leather belts are beautiful, though often expensive. Plan ahead for the winter and buy a chunky sweater or cardigan at one of the wind-battered tourist stalls selling **knitted clothes** in Fóia or Sagres. You will probably be pleasantly surprised by the prices.

A dusty bottle of **vintage port** won't break the bank and is sure to please. Beware, however, that the pretty **marzipan sweets** and fig treats may melt even the sweetest tooth.

Portuguese **pottery** is a delight, and the showrooms of Porches are full of beautiful wares, with a larger range than you will find at home. *Azulejos* are glazed painted ceramic tiles (*see* p.18), and make a good present if luggage weight is no problem.

ENTERTAINMENT AND NIGHTLIFE

For many, the beach will be the focus of daytime leisure. For those who want to get out to sea, boat trips are always fun, and for hydrophiles of a more active disposition, there are four **water parks** (*see* p.108).

After-dark entertainment in the major resorts is often high on decibels and low on charm. Albufeira and its satellites (Praia da Oura and Montechoro), in particular, are full of Europop disco-bars, and British 'fun-pubs' packed with tourists. The serious nightclubs of Kiss, Locomia and Kadoc are some way out of town. Praia da Rocha is another magnet for the '18-30' set.

At the other end of the cultural and musical spectrum is the Portuguese institution of *fado* (literally 'fate'). This haunting style of folk music is thought to

You will find fado performances at many restaurants catering for tourists.

Displays of folk dancing are guaranteed to be full of vitality, enthusiasm and colour.

have developed during the days of the Discoveries, either as a lament for men away or lost at sea, or perhaps as the song of the slaves transported aboard Portuguese vessels. A typical *fado* troupe comprises a woman dressed in black, accompanied by male guitarists. Purists are quick to point out that *fado* is not an Algarve speciality, and has its heart in Lisbon and Coimbra, but it is something all visitors should experience.

A more joyful form of local entertainment is **folk dancing**. The shows held at the Fonte Pequena (Alte) are performed largely by children, who show a genuine delight and enthusiasm in their performances. Both folk dancing and *fado* troupes also appear in hotels along the coast.

An altogether more robust diversion is

staged in the bullrings of Albufeira, Lagos, Quarteira and Vila Real every Saturday (at around 5.30pm) during the summer. There are two significant peculiarities to *tourada*, the Portuguese version of **bullfighting**. Firstly, part of the *tourada* is performed on horseback, and secondly, as the posters are keen to point out, 'The Bull is not Killed'. However, the bull, whose horns are padded is stabbed with darts until it is overcome, an will probably be killed the day after the figh Only the bravest and strongest of bulls are spared and kept for breeding purposes.

Most visitors will prefer to make their own amusement after dark, or seek out one of the **music festivals** which are staged during the summer (*see* pp.89-92). A taste of the high life may be experienced at the **casinos** of Praia da Rocha, Vilamoura and Monte Gordo. These include Las Vegas-style floorshows, which are open to all the family, though you have to be over 21 to gamble, and you will need to show your passport for identification purposes.

SPORTS

The Algarve is famous for its sporting facilities, particularly its highly rated **golf** courses, which allow top quality year-round play, just a couple of hours from the colder climes of northern Europe. If you want to play the best courses, you generally have to book well ahead, and produce proof of handicap. Some of the top courses have special booking arrangements with hotels (sometimes on site) which specialise in golfing holidays.

The grand old lady is the Penina, near Alvor, the longest and the oldest course in the Algarve. Vilamoura offers three

The famous seventh hole at Vale do Lobo.

championship courses, with Vilamoura I very highly rated. Vale do Lobo enjoys a breathtaking cliff-side setting and features 'the most photographed hole in Europe' – no 7 on the yellow course – where a good drive will carry you straight over spectacular cliffs (and a bad hook will take you down to the beach). Quinta do Lago is American-designed, with wonderful greens, roomy fairways and several water hazards. San Lorenzo is another American-designed course, which draws rave reviews but is very expensive and only open to a privileged few.

Other top-class courses to look out for are: the Alto Club, Alvor; Carvoeiro Club, Palmares, near Lagos; Parque da Floresta, Budens, near Salema (no handicap necessary); Pine Cliffs, Falésia; Pinheiros Altos, Quinta do Lago; Salgados, Praia da Galé, near Albufeira; Vale do Milho, Carvoeiro (no handicap necessary); and Vila Sol, Quarteira. Expect to pay up to 8 000 to 10 000 escudos for 18 holes.

The Algarve's gently rolling picturesque hinterland is ideal for **horse and pony trekking**, and there are many stables offering rides for all levels of experience.

Tennis coaching on the Algarve is widely available and highly rated. Big-name tutors include former British stars Roger Taylor and David Lloyd, based at Vale do Lobo and Rocha Brava (near Carvoeiro) respectively. Other venues include Vilamoura and the Ocean Club at Praia da Luz.

All the major resorts have **windsurfing** equipment for hire, but water skiing is not so popular, due to the often choppy nature of the Atlantic. Experienced windsurfers should head for Praia do Martinhal, Sagres.

The main **watersports centre** is Vilamoura, which offers just about every kind of water-based activity, including some of the best big-game fishing in Europe (along with Portimão and Sagres). Praia da Luz boasts the Luz Bay Sea Sport Centre, which claims to be Portugal's oldest diving club, and Quinta do Lago also offers excellent facilities. Dinghy sailing is popular at both.

For more aquatic fun, check out one of the water parks. The Big One (near Alcantarilha) and Slide & Splash (near

Lagoa) are probably the best in terms of thrills and spills, and provide a good half-day, especially for kids. ZooMarine, near Guia, is an amusement park based on the Florida recipe of parrots, dolphins, sea lions and sharks. Atlantic Water Park (near Quarteira) has a range of slides, rides and a high-diving show during the high season.

uatic fun at antic Water Park, ar Quarteira.

A-Z FACTFINDER

THE BASICS

Before You Go
Strictly speaking, travellers from EU countries do not need a passport to enter Portugal, but it is advisable to bring it along, particularly for drivers, who will receive an on-the-spot fine if they fail to produce it at the request of the authorities. A passport is also the only form of identification accepted at some casinos. Visitors from certain Commonwealth countries will need a visa, as will holders of British, Irish and US passports planning to stay in Portugal longer than three months.

Vaccinations are not required for visitors from Europe or North America. Travellers from areas where cholera or smallpox is present may be required to produce vaccination certificates.

Getting There
Most visitors to the Algarve travelling by air arrive at Faro Airport, which is about 15 minutes from the town, linked by bus and taxi services.
A daily train service operates between London, and Lisbon via Paris and Irun in northern Spain. The journey takes about 37 hours. British Rail operates a wide range of services to the Channel ports, and French Railways (SNCF) includes many high-speed passenger trains and motorail services throughout France. For detail contact British Rail International, Ticket and Informatio Office, PO Box 303, Victoria Station, London SW1 1JY ☎ **0171 834 2345**; French

ailways 179 Piccadilly,
ondon W1V 0BA
☎ **0171 409 3518**.

Cross-channel car and
assenger services from the
K are numerous for those
anting to drive to Portugal
approximately 2 240km/
400 miles from the French
orts to the Algarve) and there

is a car ferry service between
Plymouth and Santander – the
journey takes 24 hours – in
northern Spain (about
1 280km/800 miles to the
Algarve). There are no direct
ferry services between Britain
and Portugal.

The waterfront in Olhão.

A-Z

Accidents and Breakdowns
If you are in a hire car, the rental company should be able to assist you so carry their details with you at all times. In the event of breakdown in your own car, the Portuguese Automobile Club (Automóvel Clube de Portugal) can be called upon. Their head office is in Rua Rosa Araújo 24, Lisboa 1200 ☎ **(01) 356 3931**. Accidents should be reported to the police.

Accommodation see p.93

Airports see Getting There, p.110

Babysitters see Children

Banks
Banks are usually open from 8.30am-2.45/3pm Monday to Friday; in the larger towns and resorts a handful will probably be open later and on Saturdays. Smaller banks and those in rural areas are likely to close for lunch between 11.45am-1pm. Exchange rates vary from bank to bank, and a hefty minimum charge is levied on travellers' cheques. Many banks also have cash dispensers which accept international credit cards.

Beaches
The Algarve's 160-odd kilometres of coastline are generally clean and unpolluted and boast a number of Blue Flag beaches (commended for beach and sea cleanliness). During the high season, many beaches operate a flag safety system as follows: red flag, bathing forbidden; yellow flag, bathing with caution; green flag, safe to swim. Most beaches have at least one bar or restaurant and many of the larger resorts have a range of watersports. Nude sunbathing is forbidden on all beaches.

Bicycles
These can easily be hired from cycle-hire shops, from some car-hire firms or through the larger resort hotels. Enquire at tourist offices.

oks

ew suggested books to
nance your stay in the
arve might include:

s Vaz de Camões, *The
siads*

Iney Gallop *Portugal – A
k of Folkways*

neida Garrett *Travels in My
meland*

Read *The Moors in Spain
I Portugal*

n Ure *Henry the Navigator*

te Vieira *A Taste of Portugal*

eakdowns *see* **Accidents**

ses *see* **Transport**

mping

e Portuguese Tourist Office
olishes a list of camping and
avanning sites in Portugal,
ion by region. Both state-
hed sites and private sites,
h graded one to four stars,
listed. Camping outside
icial sites is not permitted.
international camping
net is obligatory and
oking is advisable in the
oular resorts. Further details
be obtained from the
leração Portuguesa de
mping Caravanning,
nida 5 de Outubro15–3°
00 Lisboa ☎ **(01) 315 2715**.

r Rental

rent a car in Portugal you

must be at aged least 21 years
(some companies stipulate 23)
of age and have held a full
driving licence for a year. The
rental contract, a valid driving
licence, valid vehicle insurance
and your passport must be
carried at all times. Failure to
produce any of these at the
request of the authorities may
result in an on-the-spot fine.

Cars of all sizes can be hired
all over the Algarve, both from
international and local firms,
but you should advise them in
advance if you require an
automatic. Make sure you have
comprehensive insurance and
check that the tyres, including
the spare, are in good repair
and the brakes work before
setting off. Fly-drive packages
are operated by major airlines.
See also **Driving**

Children

Children and teenagers are
well catered for in the Algarve,
where the focus is on beach
related activities. Water parks
are particularly popular.
Children under eight years of
age are entitled to a 50 per
cent discount if sharing a room
with their parents.

All baby products, both
national and imported brands,
are widely available at pharmacies and supermarkets. Larger
hotels may offer a baby-

There are many charming sights away from the busy tourist resorts, such as this farmer with his donkey.

listening service or be able to recommend local babysitters.

Churches *see* **Religion**

Climate *see* **p.89**

Clothing

The climate of the Algarve is generally hot and sunny, but it is advisable to take a sweater, even in summer, as the evenings can turn cool and some of the higher points are very blustery. Smarter clothing is expected at dinner only in some of the more expensive hotels and restaurants.

Dress Sizes

UK	8	10	12	14		16	18
Portugal	34	36	38	40		42	44
US	6	8	10	12		14	16

Men's Suits

UK/US	36	38	40	42		44	46
Portugal	46	48	50	52		54	56

Men's Shirts

UK/US	14	14.5	15	15.5	16	16.5
Portugal	36	37	38	39/40	41	42

Men's Shoes

UK	7	7.5	8.5	9.5		10.5	11
Portugal	41	42	43	44		45	46
US	8	8.5	9.5	10.5		11.5	12

omen's Shoes

	4.5	5	5.5	6		6.5	7
rtugal	38	38	39	39		40	41
	6	6.5	7	7.5		8	8.5

omplaints

ny disputes which cannot be
tisfactorily resolved on the
ot with the person in charge
ould be referred to the local
urist office.

onsulates

hese can be located at the
llowing addresses:

ustralian Embassy
enida da Liberdade
4–2 e4, 1200 Lisboa
(01) 654161

ritish Embassy
ua São Domingos à Lapa
–37, 1200 Lisboa
(01) 396 1191

ritish Consulate
argo Francisco A. Mauricio
1, 8500 Portimão
(082) 23071/27057

anadian Embassy
enida da Liberdade 144,
h Floor, 1250 Lisboa
(01) 347 4892

ish Embassy
ua da Imprensa 1,
h Floor, Lisboa
(01) 661569

S
enida Forças Armadas,
00 Lisboa
(01) 727 3300

Crime

There is no need to be unduly
concerned about crime in the
Algarve, but it is advisable to
take sensible precautions.
• Carry as little money, and as
few credit cards as possible,
and leave any valuables in the
hotel safe.
• Carry wallets and purses in
secure pockets or wear a
money belt, and carry
handbags across your body or
firmly under your arm.
• Cars, particularly hire cars,
are targeted by thieves, so
never leave your car unlocked,
and always remove any items of
value.
• If you do have anything
stolen, report it immediately to
the local police and collect a
copy of the report so that you
can make an insurance claim.
• If your passport is stolen,
report it to your consulate or
embassy at once.

Currency see **Money**

**Customs and Entry
Regulations**

The Single European market
ensures considerable tax-free
allowances for travellers from
EU countries, and there is no
limit on the transfer of goods
for personal use. Those under
17 years of age do not have an
allowance. Otherwise the limits

are as follows:
Cigarettes 800 (non EU or bought at duty-free shops 200)
Spirits 10 litres (non EU or bought at duty-free shops 1 litre)
Fortified wine 20 litres (non EU or bought at duty-free shops 2 litres)
Wine 90 litres (non EU or bought at duty-free shops 2 litres)
Beer 110 litres (EU only)

Disabled Visitors

Holidays and Travel Abroad: A Guide to Europe is available from RADAR, 12 City Forum, 250 City Road, London EC1V 8AF ☎ **0171 250 3222** (open from 10am-4pm). It contains advice and information about accommodation, transport, services, equipment and tour operators in Europe. The Holiday Care Service is available to advise British disabled people wishing to travel abroad, and can be contacted on ☎ **01293 774535.**

Tripsocope ☎ **0181 994 9294** give advice about all aspects of travel and transport for the disabled and elderly in Portugal, and can offer detailed help with planning journeys, equipment hire, etc. The Portuguese Handicapped Persons' Association is based in Lisbon at Largo do Rato, 1000 Lisboa ☎ **(01) 757 0422**.

Driving

Driving in Portugal's towns and cities can be hazardous, as the overall standard of driving here is, at best, erratic. The rules of the road are openly flouted. However, a car is often the only method of transport to some of the places off the beaten track, which really should not be missed.

When driving in Portugal you must always have with you the car's registration document (or rental contract if a hire car), a valid national driving licence (or international driving licence if you are not a member of an EU country), valid vehicle insurance (a green card is no longer compulsory for members of EU countries, but is strongly advisable if you are driving your own car) and your passport. Failure to produce any of these on request of the authorities may result in an on-the-spot fine.

Driving in Portugal is on the right-hand side and traffic approaching from the right has priority. Speed limits, clearly marked on the roads, are as follows:

• Maximum on motorways 120 kph/75 mph (minimum 40 kph/25 mph)
• Maximum in built-up areas

50 kph (31 mph)
• Maximum on other roads
90 kph (56 mph)

The police will readily impose on-the-spot fines for not wearing seat belts in the front seat and for driving while drunk.

The main roads are generally well maintained, but not all the secondary roads are as good, and motorists should be on the look-out for hazards such as pot holes and stray goats. In the event of an emergency, SOS telephones can be found at regular intervals along the main highways. Petrol is widely available in the main resorts and along the main roads but stations are few and far between in rural areas, where unleaded fuel may be particularly scarce. It is forbidden to carry a petrol can in the car. Credit cards may not be accepted at all petrol stations.

Dry Cleaning see Laundry

Electric Current
The standard current throughout Portugal is 220V, although you may still find 110V in older establishments. Sockets are the circular, two-pin variety so you will need to take an adaptor for any of your own appliances.

Embassies see Consulates

Emergencies
Police, fire and ambulance are all on the same number:
☎ 115

Etiquette
In and around the resorts there are few differences in culture that visitors need be aware of, but in the more rural areas inland, where tourists are less familiar, respect for privacy and a simpler, quieter way of

A decorated old cart.

A fishing boat beached below the fortress at Cacela Velha, east of Tavira.

life should be respected. Dress appropriately when visiting churches.

Excursions

A number of trips and tours of the Algarve are available and details of those in your area can be obtained from the local tourist office or the larger hotels. Among the options are boat trips around the coast, cruises along the Guadiana River or expeditions in a jeep through the region's more rugged countryside.

Guidebooks *see* Maps

Health

British citizens should obtain the Form E111 (avaiable from Post Offices) which entitles the holder to free urgent treatment in other EU countries. On arrival in Portugal, exchange the form a the **Segurança Social** for a book of coupons. It is advisable to take out comprehensive medical insurance.

Pharmacies *(farmácias)* are open normal shop hours (*see* **Opening Hours**) and one branch in each town remains open until late in the evening its address is posted in the

dows of all other pharma-
s and in the local news-
pers.

Most of the resorts have
glish-speaking doctors and
ntists and there are hospitals
Faro, Loulé, Albufeira,
rtimão and Lagos, where
re are English-speaking
ff.

urs see **Opening Hours**

ormation see **Tourist Infor-
ation Offices**

nguage
rtuguese is the official
guage in Portugal, but
glish, French and Spanish are
ely spoken in the Algarve. As
any country, however, an
empt at the native language
be appreciated.

Laundry
Self-service launderettes are
not common in Portugal but
the larger hotels will probably
have a laundry service and
there are many laundries to be
found; you are quite likely to
find a service even in quite
small places, operating
through the post office or local
shops.

Lost Property
Report any lost items to the
local authority, or to the tourist
office.

Maps
The *Michelin Red Guide Portugal*
provides full information on
hotels and restaurants both in
the Algarve and in Portugal,
which is useful if you are
planning to drive to the region

Good morning/**Bom dia**
Good evening/**Boa noite**
Goodbye/**Adeus**
Please/**Por favor**
Thank you (if you are male)/**Obrigado**
Thank you (if you are female)/**Obrigada**
Yes/**Sim**
No/**Não**
Do you speak English?/**Fala inglês?**
Where is .. ?/**Onde é ..?**
How much is .. ?/**Quanto é ..?**
I would like ../**Queria ...**
I don't understand/**Não compreendo**

and require overnight stops. The *Michelin Green Guide Portugal* includes detailed information on the main sights and attractions in the region, and contains town maps. Consult Michelin road maps Nos 440 (Portugal) and 990 (Spain Portugal).

Medical Care *see* Health

Money

The unit of currency in Portugal is the *escudo*, divided into 100 *centavos*. The monetary symbol is the dollar sign ($), placed between the escudo amount and the centavos, e.g., 20$50 is 20 *escudos* and 50 *centavos*. Banknotes come in denominations of 500, 1 000, 2 000, 5 000 and 10 000 *escudos;* coins in 50, 1, 2$50, 5, 10, 20, 50, 100 and 200 escudos. One thousand *escudos* is known as a *conto*.

There is no limit to the amount of *escudos* or foreign currency which may be taken into Portugal, but on leaving the country no more than 100 000$00 per person in local currency and/or travellers' cheques, and no more than the equivalent of 500 000$00 in foreign currency may be taken out. Foreign visitors entering Portugal must have a minimum of 10 000$00 (or equivalent in another currency) and a further 2 000$00 for each day of their stay.

International credit and debit cards are widely accepted in the resorts, and money and travellers' cheques can be changed at banks and many hotels (you will need your passport). Many banks also have automatic cash dispensers which accept international credit cards.

Newspapers

All major international newspapers and magazines are available on the newsstands, often on the day of publication. Useful English-language publications include *Spotlight* (which focuses on the Western resorts), and *Discover*, both of which are widely available.

Opening Hours

Shops are generally open from 9am-1pm and 3-7pm, Monday to Friday, and 9am-1pm on Saturdays. In the larger resorts some shops have longer opening hours.
Supermarkets are generally open from 8am-8pm on weekdays, with some opening on Sundays.
Markets usually start early and pack up by 1pm. Large shopping centres are open

daily from 10am-1am.
Museums and galleries are generally open from 10am-noon and from 2-5pm, although there may be local variations. Many are closed on Mondays. *See also* **Banks** and **Post Offices**

Photography

All well-known brands of film are readily available in the Algarve, and fast-processing services are equally easy to come by.

In rural areas particularly, ask permission before taking pictures of individuals. In museums and galleries, check there are no restrictions before taking photographs.

Police

The Guarda Fiscal are the police responsible for day to day law and order, traffic offences and tourist assistance. They can be recognized by their blue and grey uniforms.

The Polícia Judiciária, clad in navy blue uniforms, are concerned with violent and large-scale crime in Portugal.

Post Offices

Post offices are generally open from 9am-12.30pm and from 2.30-6pm Monday to Friday. Larger branches stay open throughout the lunch break

Look out for the characteristic filigreed chimney stacks which are found throughout the Algarve.

and are also open on Saturday mornings. *Poste restante* mail can be sent to any convenient post office. Proof of identity will need to be produced on collection.

Letter boxes and phone booths are red.

Stamps *(selos)* are sold in post offices and shops where the sign CTT Selos is displayed. It costs 75$00 to send a postcard to European countries and

95$00 to America, Australia and New Zealand.

Public Holidays
As well as the national public holidays listed below, each town celebrates the feast day of its patron saint. Tourist information centres can provide information about local holidays.

New Year's Day: 1 January
Shrove Tuesday: late February/early March
Good Friday: end March/early April
Liberation Day: 25 April
Labour Day: 1 May
National Day: 10 June
Assumption of the Virgin: 15 August
Republic Day: 5 October
All Saints' Day: 1 November
Independence Day: 1 December
Day of Our Lady: 8 December
Christmas Day: 25 December

Public Transport see **Transport**

Religion
Portugal is predominantly a Roman Catholic country and Masses are held daily in local churches. Services of most Christian denominations are conducted in English throughout the Algarve. Details can be

rise at the Ria Formosa Natural Park.

obtained from tourist offices
and larger hotels.

Smoking

Smoking is widely tolerated in
Portugal, although you will see
'No Smoking' signs in some
public buildings.

Stamps *see* Post Offices

Taxis *see* Transport

Limes ripening in the Algarve sun.

Telephones

Payphones can be found
over the Algarve. Many a
coin operated, but a large
number also take phoned
known as *credifones*. These
cards, available in 50 or 1
units, can be bought from
offices and newsstands. Y
can also call from booths
post offices, where you pa
the desk at the end of the
The cost is the same as a
payphone. Calls from ho
are much more expensive
Country codes are as foll
Australia: ☎ 61
Canada: ☎ 1
Ireland: ☎ 353
New Zealand: ☎ 64
UK: ☎ 44
USA: ☎ 1

Time Difference

From the last Sunday in
September to the last Sur
in March, Portugal obser
Greenwich Mean Time
(GMT). During the sumr
clocks go forward one ho
accordance with British
Summer Time), and so ar
hours ahead of GMT.

Tipping

In most hotels, restaurant
cafés service is already
included in the bill; if no
per cent is usual. Taxi dri
and hairdressers expect a

...er cent tip, and porters and
...otel staff are used to a small
...ratuity.

...oilets

...ublic toilets are not readily
...vailable in the Algarve, but
...hose in a bar or restaurant can
...e used by the general public,
...ut it is polite to ask first, and
...o have a drink afterwards. The
...leanest facilities tend to be in
...otels. Ladies are marked
...enhoras, and Gentlemen
...enhores, or *Homens.*

...ourist Information Offices

...ll Portuguese towns have a
...ourist information centre
...nown as Posto or Comissão de
...urismo. In the Algarve, the
...ain office is at Avenida 5 de
...utubro 18, 8000 Faro
... (089) 800400.
...ortuguese National Tourist
...ffices abroad:
...anada 60 Bloor Street West,
...uite 1 005, Toronto,
...ntario M4W 3B8
... (416) 921 7376
...eland Knocksinna House,
...nocksinna, Fox Rock,
...ublin 18
... (01) 289 3569
...K 22–25a Sackville Street,
...ndon W1X 1DE
... (0171) 494 1441
... 590 Fifth Avenue, 4th
...oor, New York, NY 10036
... (212) 354 4403/4

Tours *see* **Excursions**

Transport

LAR, a subsidiary of TAP-Air
Portugal, operates flights
between Faro and Lisbon and
the regional airports at
Oporto, Vila Real, Bragança,
Portimão, Covilhã and Viseu.

The state-run Portuguese
Railway (CP) offers a fairly
comprehensive and inexpensive service across the country.
The *rápidos* (express) are fast
and punctual – some are first-
class only; the *directos*
(intercity) are slower, make
more stops and have first and
second class compartments;
while the *regionais* (local trains)
tend to be slow and often over-
crowded.

Various discounts are
available for families and
students. Passengers over 65
pay 50 per cent of the fare, as
do children aged four to 12;
children under 4 travel free.
Special tickets and tickets with
discount should be purchased
from main line stations. It is an
offence to travel without a
valid ticket.

A motor rail service operates
between Lisbon and Oporto
and Lisbon and Faro.
A coach service operates across
the country and details of
routes and times can be
obtained from local tourist

Old wells near Silves.

offices and travel agents in Portugal.

One of the most convenient and cheapest ways of travelling around the Algarve is by bus. EVA or RODOVIÁRIA buses provide services to all the major towns and resorts. Bus stops bear the sign *paragem*.

Taxis, black with green roofs or cream coloured, are readily found in cities, resorts and many of the larger towns and villages. They are not metered and fares are based on a standard table based on mileage.

TV and Radio

The larger hotels and many bars usually have satellite television showing films and soap in their original language, plu major sporting events. Solar Radio on 94.0FM broad casts in English from 8.30am, and has regular news bulletin

Vaccinations see Before You Go, p.110

Water

It is perfectly safe to drink ta water in Portugal, but bottle mineral water is available everywhere for those who prefer it and it is always a wis precaution against stomach upsets.

Youth Hostels see Accommodation p.93

INDEX